How to get into Television, Radio and New Media

Also available from Continuum

How to Get into Advertising – Andrea Niedle
How to Get into Marketing and PR – Annie Gurton
The Guerilla Film Maker's Handbook – Chris Jones and Genevieve
  Jolliffe

How to get into Television, Radio and New Media

Mike Hollingsworth
with
Kimberley Stewart-Mole

continuum
LONDON • NEW YORK

Continuum

The Tower Building   370 Lexington Avenue
11 York Road   New York
London SE1 7NX   NY 10017–6503

British Library Cataloguing-in-Publication Data
A catalogue record for this book is available from the British Library.

ISBN: 0–8264–6731–8 (hardback)
      0–8264–6732–6 (paperback)

Typeset by YHT Ltd., London
Printed and bound in Great Britain by MPG Books Ltd, Bodmin, Cornwall

Contents

Acknowledgements

A sizeable number of people has helped me write this book – not least my sidekick and able assistant Kimberley Stewart-Mole. In the age-old tradition of awards ceremonies, however, I must thank my parents for putting me here in the first place. My dad, a lifelong military man, who died while I was preparing this book, always said that he regretted knowing little about the field of broadcasting and journalism. It meant, he said, that he could not help me in my career. I tried in vain to make him understand that his worldly advice and the fact that he gave me the freedom to 'do my thing' and be inquisitive actually made me hack my way into broadcasting in the first place. This book would have pleased him very much. On a more direct basis, I have to acknowledge the help of William Earl, Paul Campbell, Donal MacIntyre, Lowri Turner, Anne Diamond, Daryl Denham, Jon Roseman, Rob Jones, Anthony Haynes, Richard Johnson and Rebecca Hollingsworth. I also acknowledge the invaluable assistance of the Internet in tracking down a variety of detail.

How to use this book

When I first sat down to write this book, in the middle of an ever-changing broadcasting environment and with a new UK Broadcasting Bill on the immediate horizon, I asked myself this question: 'Just what does it take to get into TV, radio or the new media, now?'

That was nearly the end of the book.

The answer is that there is no single or simple answer. In today's climate, where people are literally famous for 15 minutes, you could be forgiven for believing that all you need do to get yourself in as a presenter, for instance, is to become a contestant on *Big Brother* or one of the many other reality shows that have sprung up on the broadcast horizon.

It's true that the inmates on those sort of shows seem to walk out into a hail of contracts and job offers, just for having behaved (or misbehaved?) as human guinea pigs in front of the cameras for a few weeks. However, the deeper truth is that after a few brief sparks of fame, most of the less talented zoo specimens have returned whence they came, a little bit wealthier, and a lot wiser about the other side of celebrity!

It still needs real talent to create a long-term career in broadcasting – in front of or behind the camera and microphone. It needs dogged persistence, the willingness to learn, and a large sprinkling of that luck that puts you in the right place at the right time, saying the right things.

Never was it a truer time to say: 'It's not just what you know, it's who you know – or who you can get to know...'

So, if you don't mind having your ego battered, your self-esteem shaken, your confidence tested to the utmost; if you don't mind making tea for last week's tea boy or girl, sometimes working for nothing or even paying your own way ... then stick with it. The following pages will tell you some of what you need to know in order to get a job in the best business in the world: I've been there and done it – and while I might make a few decisions differently now, most of it I wouldn't change at all!

This book is not designed to be read through like some bodice-ripping novel! It's a kit of tools and advice to enable you to pick your way through the traps and jump over the hurdles that might be put in your path to a job. I'd like you to read it all, but if, having read the first chapter, you want to skip straight to Chapter 6, Television Presenting, and then straight on to Chapter 13, How to Land a Job, then feel free! However, every page has some form of advice or tip, which you should tuck away in the back of your brain until you're ready to use it – as you inevitably will!

A Rundown of What's in the Book

The aim of this book is to introduce you to all the opportunities available for work in the modern media industry and to let you into a few trade secrets. I concentrate on three main areas: television, radio and new media.

Chapter 1 aims to introduce you to the media industry. I go on to discuss starting points such as choosing the area you wish to enter and the value of work experience. I highlight the competition that you will face in this fashionable and highly competitive field and introduce some of the jargon you will need to familiarize yourself with.

Chapter 2 concentrates on television and supplies the vital information needed by anyone who wants to work specifically in TV, be it writing, producing or presenting. Satellite, terrestrial and digital broadcasting formats as well as descriptions of the programme makers themselves are discussed, alongside all the main points of knowing the business of TV.

Chapter 3 gives the low-down on radio: local, hospital, student, community and national. The implications of digital radio, and some more jargon for your vocabulary book, are outlined as an introduction to the world of radio broadcasting.

The business of new media makes up Chapter 4, where I outline the differences between new and old media as well as the implications of interactive television and the world gone digital. I also discuss how the web has changed TV and its applications and the resulting implications, focusing particularly on how you can use your knowledge of the web to get further ahead in the media world.

Chapters 5–7 are devoted to presenting. They include tips on what makes a good presenter along with instructions and advice on how to put together a **showreel** and how to prepare for auditions. To cover the different disciplines, Chapter 5 looks at general presenting thoughts, followed by hints and tips applicable to television (Chapter 6) and then radio (Chapter 7).

Broadcast journalism and sport are the focus of Chapter 8. The move from print journalism to broadcast is quite a popular one. I also go, briefly, into how the news is put together and how you might think about journalism on newspapers or in training courses before trying for your first job in broadcasting. Sports broadcasting is a specialist area, with often takes sportsmen and women and sports journalists into its teams.

The next three chapters run through all the main jobs available in radio, TV and new media. A typical day in the studio is described with each job in its place as applied to a programme being made.

Now that you are armed with the information you need, it is time for you to get started. Chapter 12 goes through the personal skills needed to succeed in the media and skills to be learnt, such as the art of **networking**. And there are tips on how to write a format for a programme idea – which you will be expected to do when applying for most jobs in broadcasting.

How to land a job is the subject of Chapter 13 – how to put together the perfect **CV** and **cover letter** along with examples, and how to ooze enthusiasm. We'll also look at that very important skill: how to deal with rejection.

Chapter 14 gives you an explanation of the important and governing bodies in the media industry. These are the bodies that you will need to know about as you climb the ladder of success. In broadcasting, certainly, the advisory, licensing and quasi-governmental bodies have a lot to say about how you might do your job. It also contains a list of useful contacts: the sort of addresses you'll need to write to when applying for jobs. All the BBC stations and departments are included, and all the commercial stations, along with their production companies and the top independents, not forgetting their web sites.

As you go through this book you will be aware that the broadcasting industry is riddled with insider words, or jargon. Most trades and professions have their own private language, which is designed partly to act as a kind of shorthand, and partly to keep outsiders in the dark! It will help you to learn some of the jargon that is used in the business (it makes you look more like a person 'in the know'), and where I can, I highlight jargon words in bold type and provide a translation in the glossary at the back of the book. Also, for my own shorthand purposes, in several places I use the word 'broadcasting' to mean radio, television and new media.

The book is designed to be as comprehensive as space allows, so I welcome suggestions, for the next edition, of any other areas that can be included or further amplified. I would like your help in making the book even more useful for people who come after you and, as you will see at the end of the book, I offer you the chance to ask me further questions that may crop up.

Meanwhile, let's concentrate on getting you a job in the best business in the world – as they say, it beats working for a living! Enjoy reading – and good luck with the job hunt!

CHAPTER 1

So You Want to Be a Broadcaster

I Was Very Lucky

The story you're about to read tells of the luck I had in getting into the broadcast business as a raw teenager. I was 18 years old at the time of my big break and I accept totally that it was a lot easier then to make your own way in the world, find yourself a job and make your mark. These days, working in the media seems to be every other person's idea of a fun job. The competition is fierce, and I doubt whether I could follow the same route if I had to do it today. So many people are competing for so few jobs that you have to find your own special way of making your name and face stand out from the crowd. Jobs are no longer for life, like they were when I started, so qualifications and enthusiasm have to be all the more relevant. That means if you make it ... you are very special indeed.

A Bit About Me

As long ago as I can remember, I wanted to be in the **media**, although I didn't know it ... because the word 'media' had hardly been invented! The thought of being able to communicate my ideas and thoughts to hundreds, no thousands, no *millions* of people, and maybe influence the course of history, was something that thrilled me greatly. And if being famous was something I'd also have to cope with – well, I could do that too, gladly! Especially if being famous also meant being rich!

At school, I set up an illicit newspaper and sold copies to my mates and their friends. I interviewed famous people who toured to our local theatre and gave away tickets to see their shows in competitions.

The singer Cliff Richard gave me a prize for my paper, *The Star*, when he came to town, and his signed photograph was printed in every copy.

A local newspaper came to interview me about Cliff's donation, for its gossip column, and I think I asked the journalist more questions about his work than he asked me. He invited me to work with him at weekends and I took up the offer greedily. I worked part-time for him for two years, at nights and at weekends, often leaving friends' parties to telephone local darts clubs for their competition scores and then phoning them on to newspapers.

I left school dangerously early, just after doing my O-level exams at 16, but I was burning with ambition to work in the media. As soon as I could I went to work for a **freelance** journalist who'd set up his own news agency, and ended up – at the age of 17 – writing the gossip column that had first written about me!

The Big Break

We all need a break – something that will let us show our mettle to the people who matter and which will get us noticed and talked about when promotion is in the offing. Being in the right place, at the right time, can help enormously. One day, while I was a cub reporter, the phone rang and it was the BBC asking my boss if he could do a two-minute report on the bank holiday crowds in our **patch**, with details about the traffic and weather. They gave him an hour to put it together and said they'd record his report down the phone.

The report was written quite quickly but my boss suddenly decided he didn't relish the idea of hearing his voice on the radio. When the BBC rang back to record the report, he thrust the phone into my hand and ran out of the room.

I did the report instead and, minutes later, tuned in my radio to hear my youthful voice chirping back at me with news of blocked roads in the Lake District, lost mountaineers and ice-cream sellers who'd sold out of ices. Even though I was worried by my boyish tones, I burned with pride! Within minutes the phone rang with friends who'd heard me on the radio ... fame and fortune clearly beckoned. I was hooked!

A few months later I saw an advert for a **trainee** sub-editor at a television station in Norwich – Anglia TV – and, after writing off to them, I was summoned for an interview.

Dressed in my best (and only) suit I crossed the threshold of the television studio offices and nervously asked for the Programme Controller, a man called Dick Joyce, who was to influence my thinking about broadcasting for some time to come. I was ushered into his palatial offices where he took one look at me and in a gentle Norfolk voice, asked: 'My Gawd boy, how old are you? Are you old enough to work?' But after a shaky start, and a good grilling from Dick and his news editor, I was sent out of the room – only to be summoned back five minutes later to be told: 'Here you go Boy, you've got the job, for having had the cheek to apply.'

And so it was that four weeks later I once again entered that building, with my new staff card, and wearing new clothes bought for the occasion, to start life as a trainee sub-editor in the magical world of television news.

Sitting here now, more years later than I care to count, after a career that has taken me through the amazing world of television and radio, in black-and-white and colour, **am** and **fm**, on film and then on tape and now on computer-solid digital chips, doing wonderful jobs as presenter, DJ, reporter, Director of Programmes, Managing Director of radio and television companies, through to my current position as agent, company director and talent developer, I realize how lucky I was. I was in the right place at the right time, and I got in.

And so it might be for you – and if this amazing world gives you half as much pleasure as it has given me, you will have a fulfilled, funfilled, full life! Enjoy!

MIKE'S WISE WORDS – 1

At the same time as you start to read this book, start another book. Get a 'contacts book' going – keep the addresses, phone numbers and emails of all the contacts you make in there. Personal phone numbers of well-known and powerful people are like gold dust, and sometimes people pay good money just for one, ex-directory, phone number. You also need to make sure you keep a copy of all your contacts in a second place as well, such as a computer. If you were to lose your book, you could take ages building up the list all over again! And keep it to yourself ... if you are known for having a good contacts book, people will try to nick it.

Selling Yourself to the Media

Nearly every job in television and radio is highly sought after. Even if you have the best qualifications from the best university, you still have to convince people of your particular **talent** that backs up those qualifications. This same rule applies if you don't have a load of qualifications after your name, but you do have talent, drive and determination – you still have to persuade people to give you and your talent a chance in favour of someone else.

One hurdle the newcomer will face is that broadcasting appeals to so many people. The work is exciting whether you are behind the scenes or in the public eye. This ensures that every job advertized is heavily over-subscribed, making the right person for the job hard to decide upon and your chances of getting the job slimmer. Another serious problem the newcomer faces is that the vast majority of those in full-time employment are not overly keen to give way to another generation. But people do retire, and others get fired – in fact, the working-life expectancy of some broadcasters is getting close to that of some football managers!

The Competition

It's difficult to get an accurate count but I estimate that there are about 150,000+ people employed within the TV and radio industry in the UK. Many of these people are employed on a part-time basis. This is another loose calculation, but there are around 45,000 full-time media undergraduates studying in Britain today. Around 15,000 of these students graduate each year, and at least 10,000 of them apply to television and radio companies. That's just the media students. You don't need a media degree to get into broadcasting – I know theologians, historians and language graduates who are all trying to fight their way into the broadcasting arena. Add to this the graduates of film and art schools who are keen on the business. This means that there are feasibly 70,000 people applying for entry-level jobs in broadcasting every year! There are about 3000 jobs available annually. This should give you some idea of the competition. There are simply not enough jobs to go around, so be prepared for a real fight to get one; expect some knock-backs and be patient. Before embarking upon a broadcast career please sit down and think carefully – it's a tough industry.

The very first thing you need is keenness, along with determination and an obsession with how the business works. How much do you know about broadcasting? How much do you watch television and listen to radio? These are serious questions. If you've never sat and thought about how programmes are structured, why certain programmes do better than others, why some programmes are **on air** at specific times of day and who watches or listens to them, then you'd better start now.

MIKE'S WISE WORDS – 2

When people come to see me about launching their career in broadcasting, I put the vital question, 'What one programme on TV or radio that is running at the moment would you most like to work on or present?' I'm always amazed at the answers. One of the more common TV programmes among the more journalistically inclined is *GMTV*, the independent breakfast show. I think the perception is that it's exciting and gives you a chance to address constantly changing subjects. Among the under–25s it's *Blue Peter* or *How 2*, and among the radio wannabes it's evenly split between the *Chris Tarrant Breakfast Show*, Chris Evans on the radio, or Jonathon Ross. The one common feature between all the programmes is that they are live (or **as live**), and live is clearly a must for adrenaline junkies! However, the competition is fiercest for those sorts of shows, although among young people the fight for the few jobs on *Top of The Pops* must be pretty strong as well!

Where Do You Want To Be?

Taking on board that the broadcasting business has expanded enormously in recent years, what branch of it would you like to go into? TV, radio, narrowcast (cable TV/satellite), **webcasting** (where there is great expansion potential as broadband capability comes more on line)?

Also, different strokes for different folks – you want to go into broadcasting, but which bit? Music, Speech, Drama, Sport, Children's, News and Current Affairs, Documentaries, Natural History, Science – the list of **genres** is endless. You need to fit your likes and abilities to the right area. I'll help you do this later in the book.

Do Your Research!

Anyone recruiting you for a job wants hard evidence of your interest in broadcasting and a solid understanding of what is on the airwaves at the moment. You will have to prove that you know what you are talking about. Study the **schedules** (buy a good **listings** magazine), look at the **rotation** of programmes, and see how programmes are **promoted**. You should form opinions on what makes one programme good and others not so good. If you think you're heading for a job interview on a specific show, make sure you understand the programme, its history and its structure. Make sure you watch or hear the latest available edition of the show, so that you can talk

knowledgeably about the most up-to-date elements of the programme. If you can't get to see the chosen show as often as you'd like
(if it's on during the daytime, or too late at night), get someone to
tape it for you. When you view or listen to the programme, decon-
struct it, take it apart, look at the way the show works from the
ground upwards. Write out the running order, study how a show fits
together, how the items are balanced with each other, how similar
subjects are kept apart or put together, how the studio time balances
with time on film or video or how speech is balanced with music. On
radio, time the speech elements; see how the presenter has to use
minimum time to maximum effect. Feel the flow, hear how excite-
ment is generated, how the emotional balance of the show is built, get
under the skin of the person who put the show together.

Know Your Patch

If you're looking to work in a particular genre (e.g. Current Affairs or
Music), take a look at other programmes in the same group – compare
the different techniques used to present and schedule them. Which
programme appeals to which audience and why? What draws you to a
particular show? Is it the editorial stance it takes, or is it the fanciable
presenter? They both have merits.

Getting Your Foot in the Door

In Chapter 12, Getting Started, I'll illustrate for you the sort of areas
you should look at to get inside the business. Don't turn your nose up
at this – the industry is full of people who started by making the tea or
filing tapes and CDs. Zoe Ball, now a famous TV presenter and DJ,
started by being a runner in the Children's department at the BBC.
(Yes, it may have also helped that her dad, Johnny Ball, had worked
there before her, but she certainly didn't expect to slot straight in at
the top.) One of the problems you have when trying to get into the
business is making sure that your name is thought of when a good job
comes up. Most employers will tell you 'We'll keep you in mind',
which sometimes means 'Your CV was just filed in the bin'. They
forget you as soon as they have something else to think about. Zoe
Ball was 'in their face' all the time, and when it came to the search for
a new presenter there she was working in the office! Anthea Turner,
also now famous, started as the librarian at Signal Radio in her home
town of Stoke on Trent before graduating to the ranks of DJ, and then
on to bigger and better things in national television. The vacant job of
librarian at Signal Radio was taken by her sister Wendy, now well
known as a presenter of animal programmes on Channel 4.

The lesson of all these examples is that they got their foot in the door. It allowed them to look around at the jobs that were there when they fell vacant. **Work experience** also does exactly that – it fits you for the next stage, and when you get to the job interview you know what you're talking about.

MIKE'S WISE WORDS – 3

Don't underestimate the value of working (without pay) even for a few days in a broadcast organization or an associated company. Apart from the obvious value of getting to see the inside story, you also get to view the variety of jobs that are available (which helps you to decide the direction you want to go). Furthermore, you will be able to gain some valuable contacts (make sure you fill up your address book while you're there), and it gives you something to show you're interested in the business. Later in the book I'll be discussing how, even for beginners' jobs, a prospective employer will be looking for evidence of real interest in the broadcast industry – and you can show this by making sure that you get to spend some **work experience** time in the holidays or at weekends doing something to put on your CV.

Jargon

When I was a fledgling journalist, I soon learned that the way to get into the vicinity of any good story was to pick up some of the associated jargon. It makes you seem part of the furniture, an insider if you like, and it avoids you sticking out like a sore thumb as you ferret around for vital information for your scoop. The same is true of getting into the broadcast game. If you can sprinkle your conversation, especially at job interviews, with some juicy bits of jargon – like **VT** (video tape), **Cap Gen** (Caption Generator), **Harry** (graphic editor), **TVC** (BBC Television Centre), **Dish Farm** (Satellite Uplink Centre) etc. – it all helps you to bluff or bullshit your way through interviews and similar encounters. You have to remember that other people are doing the same thing, so keep up! Make sure, however, that you know what the jargon means – you don't want to flash words like **Pangalactic gargle blaster** around and suddenly find you're foot-faulted because you're talking to the person who invented it!

Getting In

If, after this illustration of how to shape up, you're still determined to get into this risky, demanding, but fun business, remember this: so are lots of other people. Many will look and sound the same as you; they'll have the same skills and the same qualities. You have got to find a way of standing out from the crowd and be original. This will have to shine through in your appearance, your demeanour, your application and your performances. Always try to find something different. Thousands of people apply for jobs, only a few get through to the final interviews. To make sure it's you, think about how they will remember you separately from the others. More tips on this later.

Broadcasting is made up of many tiny compartments, but whether you choose to work in television, radio or the relatively infant world of new media it all comes together as part of the world of communication, entertainment and information. The convergence of different mediums is helping to build a different world, and a really exciting one in which to take part.

So What Do We Know Now?

- *You make your own luck*
- *You must get the right qualifications together*
- *The business is changing all the time – keep well briefed*
- *The competition is fierce – make yourself stand out*
- *Have a clear mind on where you want to be*
- *Do your research*
- *Work without pay to get your foot in the door*

Knowing the Business

CHAPTER 2

Television

Fact or Fiction?

Television productions divide into two distinct areas, with a little bit of grey in between. It's what I call fact or fiction: fiction is all those things that rely on performances – Drama, Comedy, Series, Game shows, etc.; fact is everything that relies on the positive delivery of factual information – News, Science, History, Quizzes etc. In between you have a small area, which has been labelled Factual Entertainment, and which, in a sense, is what it says – making entertainment out of factual material – as in breakfast television, mid-morning magazine shows, audience discussions, etc. You need to decide which of these camps your talent falls into and where your ambition should take you. Fact is very journalistic; fiction is very arty and showbizzy – and the bit in the middle can take people from either side.

I have separated the three component elements of television, radio and new media in the next three chapters because each of them requires slightly different skills and interests, although they all lean on each other and people often cross between the different areas. Radio is the oldest medium, from the days when people would don a pair of tinny headphones and play with a 'cat's whisker' and a crystal to hear station 2LO in London, to the current plethora of stations giving different services all over the country. New media is what it says – new. It's the way in which the computer has integrated with the old broadcast systems to create a new way of delivering entertainment and information. Television is the one medium which has probably affected most people's lives and is singled out as the most exciting work area in the broadcast business.

What You Need to Know about TV

It's vital, if you are aiming for a job in the television business, to know something of how it is structured. It isn't good enough just to know that you enjoy watching the programmes of ITV or Channel 5 to lay claim on a job there. You need to know where the company fits into the whole picture, how their programmes are made, and what part you might want to play

The main activities of TV stations include the **production** and **acquisition** of programmes to fill a broadcasting schedule. The sort of programmes that a station broadcasts depends on the target audience and tone of the station – rather like in newspapers, where the *Sun*'s front page is almost certainly going to be different from that of, say, the *Daily Telegraph*; they have different priorities and appeal to different 'audiences'.

The Power Base

It is important to recognize where the power lies in the broadcast industry. The **terrestrial** broadcasters (the five main television structures) still call most of the shots. Between them they spend around £2.5 billion per year.

The BBC had television all to itself from around 1936, suspended activities through the Second World War and came back on again in time to broadcast Queen Elizabeth's coronation in 1953, which really set its popularity going. In 1954 the monopoly of the BBC, with its metropolitan bias, was broken with the introduction of independent television **ITV**, a commercial television system that was regionally based. Stations opened first in London, then Manchester and Birmingham; before long Glasgow, Northern Ireland and Cardiff followed and others afterwards.

The ITV stations were controlled largely by existing interests such as the big theatre entertainment companies, or newspaper barons. One such baron, Lord Thomson, famously made the mistake of telling the world how lucrative the early commercial stations were by announcing that, with Scottish Television, he had won a 'licence to print money'. In later years, as the industry came under heavier governmental control, and then more '**spectrum**' became available, leading to more channels, the licence to print money was looking a little dog-eared.

The BBC and commercial stations are now challenged by the various **digital** and **satellite** stations, Sky, CNN, **generic** sports channels and generic children's channels such as Nickelodeon, Disney and Trouble, among others. In recent times terrestrial broadcasters have ventured onto satellite too with spin-offs like E4 and Film Four (Channel 4), ITV2 and so on. This has served to counter the challenge issued by the satellite stations.

We must also look at the independent production companies who supply these major companies with programmes. Some of these are just 'one person and a dog'; others like, say, Endemol (*Big Brother*) and Tiger Aspect (*Blackadder*, *The Vicar of Dibley*) are growing bigger and more powerful.

MIKE'S WISE WORDS – 4

Although not everyone working in programming will necessarily be involved in the technical side of sending the programme out to the viewers, it is important to understand the systems of transmission currently in use. Developments in transmission will affect the way we make programmes in the future. (This is also where the jargon of the business starts to bite – learn the jargon words, they're good for bluffing, especially in job interviews.) **Interactivity**, especially, will make quite serious changes in the way we think about and use television, and the TV producers of the future will use two-way communication with their audience without a second thought.

Terrestrial Broadcasting

This term really refers to pictures conveyed by land-based transmitters. BBC 1, BBC 2, ITV, Channel 4 and Channel 5, plus most radio stations, can be received in this way without the use of a special dish or receiver. It is the way in which TV and radio were originally transmitted back in the mists of time – a system known as **analogue**.

The UK is switching to a different form of transmission – **digital**. The set top boxes which receive digital signals are in about half the homes in the UK and are said to be a more robust and clear way to receive pictures and sound. Instead of the analogue signals, which were sent to the TV aerial by a continuously varying electronic signal, the digital signal is received and converted to picture and sound in the form of binary digits (similar to computer language). The result of all this, they say, is a clearer picture on screen, clearer sound from your speakers and less chance of interference.

Terrestrial transmission is gradually switching to digital, and eventually analogue transmitters will be switched off.

Satellite Broadcasting

Obviously, this is transmissions from satellites, which hover in a seemingly static (**geo-stationary**) position above the earth. Television signals are beamed up to each satellite, which has a number of re-transmitters (**transponders**), which beam the pictures back to earth over the UK. Each transponder has a reception area (**footprint**) back on Mother Earth and anyone within the footprint can receive the TV or radio station. A large number of satellite TV and radio stations can be received in the UK, mainly as part of the package system known as Sky TV (although not all the TV stations in the package are owned by Sky, or BSkyB as it is also known). The actual satellites beaming signals to the UK are operated from Luxembourg, although most of the programmes are **uplinked** from a satellite **dish farm** in London's Docklands.

Satellite television and radio is also in the process of switching to digital – in fact, it is currently ahead of the terrestrial system. To receive the satellite signal you need a small dish aerial and a **set top box**. Gradually the set top boxes are being incorporated into receivers. You also need to pay a subscription.

The British digital system not only allows for more stations to be received on your radio or TV set, it also allows for **interactivity** to occur – where the viewer can send information back to the broadcaster. Interactivity has already affected the way some programme makers construct their programmes, for instance, by allowing viewers to select the outcome of a drama, or to choose the cameras they can watch from at a football game, or to elect someone to be thrown out of the *Big Brother* house. It will have a greater and greater effect on the structure of television and radio as time goes on. You will need to think carefully about how it can be used – and job interviews will ask for your ideas on this!

The Programme Makers

The BBC

The two major BBC channels, and now BBC 3 and 4, BBC News 24, and Cbeebies, are primarily funded by licence fees paid by the public: the **TV licence**. BBC Television was founded in 1936 (it was the only channel available for some 18 years), and it was also the channel which brought the nation together for such events as the Coronation of Queen Elizabeth II and the funeral of Sir Winston Churchill. It is interesting that with the recent death of the Queen Mother and the Golden Jubilee of Elizabeth II, the BBC still ran away with the top viewing figures – it is still, for many, the trusted 'voice' of Britain.

BBC 2 came on air in 1964 with a more specialist view on broadcasting aiming to serve audiences interested in art, music, sport, politics and history rather than the drama, movies and documentaries of BBC 1. Most programmes that achieve high viewing figures on BBC 2 are moved across to BBC 1, such as *One Foot in the Grave* and *Have I Got News For You* ... . Both channels were founded to provide a public broadcasting service with learning and entertainment high on the agenda.

ITV

In a state of flux at the time of writing, ITV – or Channel 3 as it once called itself – was made up of 15 different companies, each of which was awarded a licence to broadcast in a particular region. Licences used to be awarded to the companies which, in the view of a government-appointed body, made the best proposal for each region. However, after the 1991 **franchise 'auction'**, the licences were effectively sold to the highest bidders and, soon after, became the target for takeovers. In recent proposals, it appears that much of ITV may become owned by one company, in England and Wales at least, and end up being controlled centrally. GMTV, the breakfast TV station, does not have a region of its own. It has a time zone instead – 6 a.m. to 9.25 a.m. – and it broadcasts on the whole of the ITV network.

The same legislation that could create one ITV station should also provide for local output to be maintained, which means that regional newsrooms and regional feature programmes will still be good places in which to start a broadcasting career.

Channel 4

Since 1982, Channel 4 has been the television channel that is briefed to provide 'originality and diversity'. It is a publicly owned and self-funding (through advertising) broadcaster that makes very few programmes of its own, but controls its output through Commissioning Editors who **commission** or buy in programmes from independent companies. The channel attempts to be in the lead in terms of innovation and the exploration of new television boundaries. Sometimes it succeeds, sometimes it fails – but then, the right to fail is its most important prerogative. It aims to be the most creative and stimulating place to work in British television and it is strong on learning culture. It currently aims at a younger audience, and its programmes earn it a considerable amount of criticism from the more staid elements of the press.

S4C

Since 1982, all Welsh language TV programmes, from whatever source, have been transmitted on S4C to create one comprehensive Welsh service. Prior to S4C's establishment, the limited number of Welsh programmes produced were scattered throughout BBC and ITV schedules.

Over the years, S4C has developed a distinctive role in the provision of public service broadcasting to a bilingual community. More recently, new technology, such as the advent of digital television in 1998, has enabled S4C to extend that role by setting up other services.

Like Channel 4, S4C is a commissioning broadcaster, rather than a programme producer. It aims to create jobs and boost the local economy throughout Wales. All the services on offer are transmitted from S4C's headquarters in Llanishen, Cardiff. Some of the country's richest independents serve this Welsh channel – they gain their extra income by selling on their programmes re-dubbed into other languages.

S4C has an obligation to broadcast a majority of Welsh language output during peak viewing hours (6 p.m. to 10 p.m.). The schedule provides a wide variety of popular TV – drama, entertainment, sports, music, news and current affairs, games and quizzes, youth and children's programming.

S4C 2

S4C 2 is a digital channel, launched in September 1999, providing live coverage of the work of the National Assembly for Wales.

If you want a job on either of the S4C channels, it would pay to be bilingual!

Channel 5 (five)

In 1991, the governing body of commercial television (the ITC) said it could be persuaded that there was need for a further terrestrial channel. A number of groups came forward with proposals, but it wasn't until some years later that Channel 5 emerged as a viable proposition. It began broadcasting in 1997 and now reaches about 80 per cent of the homes in the UK.

Recently, Channel 5 has re-branded itself as five, and has attempted to move 'upmarket' by commissioning more factual programmes and arts programmes. It also has a news service, run by ITN, that is regarded as innovative and directed towards a more thirty-something audience. It is a general entertainment channel and is bidding strongly to compete with ITV and BBC 1. It is the first major terrestrial television channel to be controlled by a non-UK company – in this case RTL, the German/French broadcaster based in Luxembourg.

MIKE'S WISE WORDS – 5

As well as climbing the ladder within television, you can let the ladder rise underneath you. Get in on the ground floor of a completely new operation. There's nothing quite like being in at the beginning of a new channel or programme. The opportunities are greater, and because it's new there are fewer people around who have made their mark. When the programme or channel is a success, so you and your talents are that much more in demand by others. This happened for my client, Kirsty Young, who agonized long and hard over whether to join Channel 5 (now called Five) when it started in 1997. As her agent, I was criticized by a number of colleagues who thought I was mad to have her move from the BBC. But she joined and, when the press acclaimed the new style of news presentation that she spearheaded, Kirsty's star rose in the firmament!

Restricted Service Licence (RSL) TV

Relatively little is known, on a national basis, about a number of television licences that were handed out in the late 1990s to allow television broadcasting on a very local basis. There are several stations on the air in different parts of the UK that have analogue terrestrial licences allowing them to broadcast to a particular locality. Some of the licence-owners have joined together to form mini-networks and they have small production units – often voluntary – providing local news and feature programmes to their own community. These licences are granted on a four-yearly basis, but most of the RSL companies appear to be confident that they are guaranteed to carry on for a lot longer if they behave well.

These stations are ideal for getting your first experience of working in a television environment. Because many depend on voluntary or low-paid help, they are particularly vulnerable to enthusiastic starters! No plans have been revealed yet about what happens to the RSLs when the analogue transmitters are switched off.

Information about your nearest RSL broadcaster can be obtained from Ofcom or the ITC residual body (for contact details, see Chapter 14).

Programme Making

The programme making and broadcasting sections of television companies are becoming more and more separate and it is important that you understand which section you are applying to. The main broadcasters have been listed in the previous section. Most of these will have some form of **in-house** programme production capability. In the case of Channels 4 and 5 that is quite limited, as they commission mainly from outsiders. The BBC, however, produces, commissions and acquires programmes to broadcast. This involves a large number of people and a diverse range of jobs.

There is a group of people at the top who decide what sort of programmes will be shown, where in the day and in the week they will go, whether they will be a one-off, a series, live or pre-recorded, and if they will be made in house or by an independent production company.

The BBC is split into programme departments: Drama, Entertainment, Children's, Factual, Arts and Music. There are then subsections of each department, i.e. people in drama are split into those who deal with serials, series, or one-off specials. Each programme department is given a budget, a number of programme hours to fill and a series of deadlines by which programmes must be ready for transmission.

Take **in-house** drama as an example. A script will be commissioned, by the drama department, from an independent scriptwriter or a BBC scriptwriter. The script will then be approved, redrafted, edited and from there the production starts to expand. Actors will need to be employed and contracted, costumes designed and made, locations figured out. All the people involved in such a production work under a producer.

A director needs to be found to take care of the artistic side of things, while the producer manages the production. Rehearsals begin before it is performed and then filmed or videotaped. The tape is then edited and a **final cut** approved. It goes through **post-production** and then is given its broadcast slot.

The BBC employs approximately 20,000 people, many of them directly involved in programme production. Many of the jobs at the BBC are advertised internally – and if you can get through security to view some of the job advertisement boards, you'll be amazed at the wide range of employment available.

Another way to get an inside view is to get hold of a copy of *Ariel*, the BBC's in-house newspaper, which carries all the jobs both internal and external. *Ariel* comes out every Thursday and is left in special distribution bins near reception in many of the BBC's main buildings. And don't forget that the BBC advertises many of its production jobs in the *Guardian* media pages every Monday, and occasionally in broadcast and radio magazines and on the web. Just looking at the list of jobs available helps you to form a picture of the scope of the organization. More BBC jobs low-down later in the book.

Commercial companies have spent a lot of time dividing the broadcast and production sections of their operations. The Broadcast section will have under its wing the physical bits of machinery that are needed to feed a programme signal out to the transmitters, e.g., transmission and continuity suites. This section will also usually be responsible for the local programmes that are part of the licence conditions, e.g., news and other local output – in fact, anything which is necessary to comply with the broadcast licence agreement. Anything else, such as Granada's *Coronation Street*, or Yorkshire TV's *Emmerdale*, is counted as production and will be produced under that department. These ITV production departments work virtually as independent producers and, although they may be in a favoured position when it comes to selling their product, the budgetary guidelines are now very similar. Be sure, when you are writing for a job, which department or company is producing the show you want to work on!

Often local programmes will be a good way in, since each company has to produce a specific number of hours of output and the work is always there. Also, because the daily programme output is set to a particular schedule, the routines for producing the programme are well established and easier to learn. You don't have to be a journalist to work in the local news or sports departments – but it does help.

Independent Production Companies
In addition to seeking work with the BBC or commercial companies, where competition is fierce, it is also worth looking at independent companies who specialize in the programming areas in which you are interested. Such companies are often set up by specialized producers and vary from quite basic administrative set-ups to massive world-wide companies selling programmes across Europe and the Atlantic.

In the UK the Independent sector is co-ordinated by an organization called **PACT** (Producers Alliance for Cinema and Television), and a glance at the PACT Directory (see the contacts section, Chapter 14) will show you the wide variety of independent producers that exists. These producers often have vacancies on a short-term basis for production teams, when they suddenly find themselves with a commission. Adverts tend to appear in the places previously recommended, and on a number of web sites that are also listed towards the end of the book.

MIKE'S WISE WORDS – 6

Remember, if you go to join a small independent production company the key factor for them in any commission is making it come in on budget. Profit margins are squeezed tightly by commissioning television companies and, therefore, companies will only take on staff that they know can produce the goods at the cheapest possible price. The best way into an independent is as a runner or part-time helper; research work in independents (which is the start point of any production ladder) is usually given to experienced researchers. This is one of those jobs where you might have to work for nothing for a while to get going.

Programmes and Categories

Celebrity-led quiz and chat shows, stand up and situation comedies. These sorts of programmes provide the entertainment and escapism that most people require from television. Production budgets are often high in this area; the broadcaster needs to sell you, the viewer, on a series, every Thursday at 8 p.m. for example, rather than on a one-off movie or documentary. Star talent costs money, as do the production requirements.

Most light entertainment is produced in Britains for Britains, to the British sense of humour. The occasional show will find its way across the Channel or the Atlantic. Rowan Atkinson's *Mr Bean* did okay in Europe, probably largely due to the fact that it was practically a silent movie. *Absolutely Fabulous* has found a fan base across the pond, as did *The Weakest Link* and *Who Wants to be A Millionaire*, but such cases are few and far between. America is a very self-centred market and because of the size of the potential audience out of 250 million viewers, they can spend more on production values than many shows over here, which are bidding for a slice of a much smaller cake. *Friends*, for instance, takes a long time to produce. It has teams of writers and an audience sometimes has to sit through six to ten hours of recording while the writers re-vamp scripts after seeing how well they are received. That doesn't happen often in the UK.

Entertainment shows are those programmes that are shown purely for fun: quizzes, chat shows, situation comedies and movies. So a broadcaster, when putting together a Saturday schedule, will fill it with as much fun as possible with the idea that people will conclude that it is easier to stay in and watch television than to go out and seek fun for themselves. Such scheduling is very difficult; the Entertainment department has to keep up-to-date with the fashions of the young and old to appeal to as many as possible. If you look back at the last ten years of BBC Saturday nights, you will see a steady and predictable mix of a game show, now the national lottery, a familiar, non-taxing drama such as *Casualty*, and a nice chat show such as *Parkinson*. Sometimes they will finish off with a popular movie but rarely will you spot a current affairs programme or wildlife documentary on a Saturday night. They have their rules, which are known to work.

Documentaries and fact-based or educational programming and news programmes all have their place, but not usually in the peak time part of the schedules – although the rule is often broken. Documentaries, including natural history, often use a celebrity to link the programme in order to give a subject popular appeal. That puts programmes like Michael Palin's *Around the World in 80 Days* straight into peak time. News will sometimes move temporarily into peak time if a particular event captures the public imagination, such as the death of Princess Diana, or an international war. Mainly, though, these sorts of shows will have their own slots on the edges of peak. A certain amount of controversy has been stirred up by the moving of *Panorama*, once described as a **flagship** programme of the BBC, to a late night Sunday position, where only viewers who specifically want to see it will make an appointment to watch. Programmes like *Panorama* are often quite labour-intensive and take some time to produce, because of the need for checking facts and making sure that the material is legally sound. Sometimes an **undercover** production team can spend hours waiting for the right material for their documentary. The expense of producing a costly documentary can often be compared unfavourably with a show that can be bought in at a fraction of the cost and produce a larger audience.

Factual shows can, though, be extremely rewarding to work on, as they sometimes expose scandal in governments or companies and result in changes in the law or social structure, and can affect the way we live our future lives. One such documentary, made for the ITV series *This Week*, was about the sudden cot death of my young son Sebastian Diamond. Sebastian, or 'Supi' as the family called him, died after being put to sleep on his front as the health booklets of the time recommended. A feisty producer called Linda MacDougall discovered that the recommendation was wrong and that, in her home country of New Zealand, they had found that putting a baby to sleep on its front was a possible cause of cot death.

My then wife Anne Diamond and I made a film with Linda, called 'Every Mother's Nightmare', which exposed the scandal of government inaction over cot deaths in the UK. Eighteen hundred babies a year were dying from this strange affliction. After the programme was broadcast, the government hastily withdrew the health booklets and issued new guidance on the treatment of young babies. Our 'Back to Sleep' campaign resulted in the death rate dropping to below four hundred a year. It never brought back our beloved Supi, but it saved the lives of countless unborn children.

Television can be a powerful medium – whether it is used to campaign in the way I've illustrated, to make political points, to educate us about all aspects of our daily lives, to bring us pictures of world happenings, or simply to entertain us, engage us and make us laugh and enjoy our lives in a more exciting way. Working in television is exciting and engaging too – and you can often make a difference to the lives of others while you work!

So What Do We Know Now?

- *Choose your destination – fact or fiction*
- *Learn about the whole business – not just the bit you fancy*
- *Think about working on new programmes and channels – promotion can be quicker*
- *Independent production companies can be strapped for cash – pay may be low*
- *Television is a powerful medium for getting your message across*
- *Think about lateral chances – and utilize all your skills*

CHAPTER 3

Radio

The Senior Service

Radio is the oldest form of human broadcasting, i.e., using the human voice rather than paper. However, it has no reputation for being old fashioned and continues to attract young people with the same enthusiasm as TV does. Radio has managed to evolve to survive through technological advancements and is now relied upon for news, traffic updates and weather reports in a way that TV is not. In a traffic jam the radio is your only companion, in hospital it is the same, and in the middle of the night when the whole world appears to be asleep your radio with the late-night broadcaster's soothing voice is your sole companion.

Although it might now be looked upon by some as a 'poor relation' of television, radio in the UK has a proud history and plays a major role in the community life of the country. Radio is often looked upon as a stepping-stone into television, but with the success of the likes of Chris Tarrant, Steve Penk and Cat Deeley, more and more people are regarding it as an opportunity in itself.

What You Need To Know

The radio business in Britain really started to boom with the launch of commercial radio in the early 1970s, but, of course, the BBC had been running stations since the 1920s, which is when the very first station at Savoy Hill in London (2LO) went on the air.

Commercial radio, **ILR** (independent local radio) started in Britain in 1972, with the launch of the two London stations LBC and Capital. Now there are over two hundred commercial terrestrial radio stations of all shapes and sizes, serving communities large and small up and down the country. You can read more about them and their supporting organizations in Chapter 14.

Unlike TV, radio stations mainly construct their own programmes – even adverts – although there are a number of highly competent independent radio production companies and support service companies, including **IRN** (Independent Radio News) transmitter operators, promotions companies and content information providers. I use the word 'construct' when referring to radio programmes because many stations in this country depend on pre-recorded music, on CD, to entertain their listeners. A large part of their output consists of playing copies of other people's creative work, and sometimes they appear to forget the huge debt they owe to the singers and musicians whose work they use.

MIKE'S WISE WORDS – 7

There is more freedom in working in radio than working in television, where there is a firm structure and strict hierarchy. Some people see radio as television without pictures and vice versa, but they are completely different mediums and without having the pictures there you can actually explore lots of different ideas purely with words. You can cover a broader range of topics in one show because you can interview all sorts of different people and not have to worry about how they look or whether their clothes clash with the background or with each other! It's just voices, and the listener makes his or her own impression and visualization of what you're talking about.

While recent radio history has seen an explosion in the number of radio stations around the country, it has also seen a contraction in the number of people required to run a station. For example, 15 years ago a high-ranking mid-morning independent radio show would have needed a producer, an engineer, a researcher, a phone operator and a presenter. Now the modern producer would take on some research, the researcher will cover the phones and the presenter will **drive the desk** in the absence of an engineer. In many smaller stations the presenter does the lot – and if the breakfast presenter doesn't get up, the station doesn't go on air!

Although people working in programming are not that concerned about the technical aspects of the business, it is necessary, because of the changing nature of the methods of transmission (or **platforms**), to understand the systems in use.

Terrestrial Radio Broadcasting

The term 'terrestrial' refers to sound conveyed by land-based trans-mitters. Despite attempts to jerk listeners into using **digital** (computer-like binary transmission) receivers, most radio is still listened to in **analogue** form (in which the sound is conveyed by varying the electronic signal through the transmitters).

The BBC runs five national analogue terrestrial channels: Radio 1, which plays new popular music; Radio 2, older popular music and some chat; Radio 3, classical music; Radio 4, which is mainly speech; and Radio 5, which carries news and sport. Two other stations – Radios 6 and 7 – are available on digital systems, explained later.

There is then a chain of 44 BBC local radio stations up and down the country. They differ in output according to the locality they serve and, although they do play a lot of music, the emphasis in content is on local news, information and community speech. Of the stations, 38 are strictly local radio, in territories throughout England. There are then six other stations serving Ireland (three), Wales (two) and Scotland.

The commercial local stations are companies who hold licences as a result of putting forward proposals to run a radio service. Some of the local stations are owned by the same companies and have been formed into groups (e.g., Classic Gold, Galaxy, GWR), which makes them virtually national networks. The licences are awarded to the company whose proposals are judged the best by a government-appointed body (first it was the IBA, then the Radio Authority and now Ofcom). The method of awarding licences may change: some say that the American method of just allowing stations to go on the air and letting the fittest survive is the best idea, but there are no plans to change yet.

There are also three national commercial radio stations – TalkSport radio (which concentrates on talk about sport and other subjects mainly of interest to men), Classic FM (popular classical music) and Virgin Radio (national popular rock music) – where their licences were bought by their owners in an auction of frequencies.

Digital Radio

As I said earlier, the government has recently introduced a system of digital radio (or **DAB**). The digital system translates each sound into a rapid sequence of binary digits, which are converted back to analogue before they reach the radio speakers. Analogue simply uses electronic circuits to mimic sound directly.

Digital radio relies on a chain of digital transmitters, or **multi-plexers**, some operating on a national basis, some on a local. All of the multiplexers are capable of carrying many more services than the old analogue system and so there are a considerable number of radio stations being broadcast on digital that are yet to gain a substantial audience. Digital requires a special receiver, and these are only just coming into a price range that will allow many more people to buy them. In the UK digital radio uses one of the seven frequencies available in the range 217.5–230 MHz. These are known as frequency blocks.

The operators of these digital multiplexers can also adjust the number of stations being broadcast from time to time, by varying the **bandwidth** that each station is carried on within their allocated spectrum. This means that you can have ten stations broadcasting regularly and then on, say, Saturday, one station can split into two services to provide coverage of two different sporting events that are on at the same time. The system also allows for coded reception, so that pay-radio services are possible, and a considerable amount of extra information can be carried with each signal. This means that your radio can tell you, on a small screen, what music is being played at any one time, by which artist, etc. They'll be broadcasting pictures with radio next – maybe they'll call it television!

Satellite Radio

Most people know about television channels that can be received from satellites, which are positioned in a stationary position above the earth. The companies which run these services also transmit radio channels. On the **Sky** system, which is the most favoured satellite package in Britain, there are a number of radio stations available. Some of them are existing channels, such as the BBC stations and the commercial national channels; others are specially set up for satellite distribution only. There are also private radio networks being broadcast by satellite on coded channels – several of the big store chains have their own radio networks which are re-broadcast on the loudspeaker systems in-store (Homebase, Virgin Megastore, etc.).

Prospects

Job opportunities in radio are considerably greater than those in television. The BBC, being a national corporation, prefers to recruit through training programmes, but managers of its local radio stations do have some freedom to employ people on a freelance basis. It is always worth enquiring whether they have any opportunities, on the principle that any experience is better than none.

Though many of the commercial stations are now owned by large groups they are always on the lookout for young presenters and are often willing to give experience, sometimes unpaid, to eager young people, though the chances to get behind a microphone are likely to be greater in community stations, which are often manned by volunteers and operate on very small budgets. The same applies to hospital radio, which is invariably run solely by volunteers. Any experience of broadcasting is useful, both for the development of your career and to put on your CV, and there are a number of nationally known presenters who began in very humble and sometimes unpaid capacities on local stations.

Those who are high up in radio today have made it happen for themselves. Nobody has kicked off their career presenting a top-class national breakfast show (the breakfast show is generally regarded as the most important and most listened-to show on the station, and so it's the top job). Get as much experience as you can, if possible while you are still in education. I feel there is a danger in graduating from university and then starting on your work experience, which shows a prospective employer that you didn't think about what you wanted to do in your formative years. However, if you do too much voluntary work at this stage then you are in danger of suggesting that you can work for free; people will be more reluctant to pay you for your time if they think they can get it for nothing. You have to strike a happy medium – not easy, but you can do it! Becoming a successful radio broadcaster is never simply down to the myth of a lucky break. If you have already graduated, or if going into broadcasting is a mid-life career change for you, do not despair – get your experience when you can; the advice in this book should be relevant to the broadcasting enthusiast regardless of age. A prospective employer from a radio station will favour a candidate who has already been introduced to the radio studio, desks and microphone. Pure academic theory, whilst useful, is not enough. Chapter 12 discusses the values of and how to get work experience.

MIKE'S WISE WORDS – 8

When BBC local radio first started, I was on the team that opened the first ever radio station – in Leicester in November 1967 – and I was able to move up the promotional ladder quite quickly. One of the 'problems' faced was that many people then working in the BBC did not want to transfer to local radio – they regarded it as 'beneath' them. So it gave an opportunity to others which hadn't been available for many years – an easier route into the BBC. Many local people were recruited to join BBC local radio stations and have made terrific careers, after pestering the local station manager to let them work. People who are now nationally famous household names started their careers on local radio – especially in the sports world. Also, the sudden need for people meant that individuals from all walks of life became full-time broadcasters, and to my recollection those who made it really well were teachers and clergy (used to talking for a living!). One of the radio industry's very top executives, Ron Coles, was a trainee teacher in Leicester when he took up his microphone and talked! So, whatever you are doing now – remember, you could be the top banana tomorrow!

Programme Making

Radio output can be divided into two areas: music based and speech based. These two areas sub-divide again, into different forms of music and different forms of speech. Once upon a time, you could receive a radio station that sounded very much like one of the main television channels – a mixture of all different forms of entertainment, music and information. Now, however, each station fits a particular **genre** and attracts a particular audience, although many listeners like to flit between their choice of music station and selected speech station.

BBC

The single largest provider of radio in Britain is the BBC, which broadcasts both nationally and locally. It produces radio right across the genres: punch a button and you get your selected form of radio entertainment.

Radios 1 and 2 are produced in roughly the same way, even though the music they play is different. Basically, the 24-hour day is split into **day parts** and a (sometimes self-operating) presenter (or disc-jockey, DJ) will occupy each day part. Each show depends very much on the personality and versatility of the presenter, interleaving their comments and banter around the music. The music is selected from a **playlist,** which is decided by the station's controller, and a certain amount of flexibility is given to the producer of each show to programme the music. Very rarely now are presenters allowed to select their own music. The amount of talking a presenter will do varies according to the style of the show, but the amount of music generally played in each programme, compared to the speech content, is very high.

As I have said, the most important part of the day for the popular music channels is the breakfast show and, in recent years, the market value of the breakfast show presenter has escalated. Rumours about salaries put breakfast presenters' income into the £million bracket – and when you see the popular following that some presenters can attract, you understand why their market value is so high. Another trend in recent years has been for presenters (especially on breakfast shows) to surround themselves with a team or 'posse' of people, who chip in with remarks and are the butt of sly comments and jokes. Each member of the posse will have a specific job, like weather or travel presenting, as well. This team effort is known as the **zoo format**.

The popular music channels also carry news and information, which is produced by the BBC from a central source and then customized to suit the style of each channel. Radio 1 has a special news show of its own. Radio 2 carries more news items and interviews in some of its programmes.

BBC Radio 3 is almost exclusively classical music, although it does carry speech and has broadcast 'world music' programmes as well. It too has its own customized news service, and if a world-famous composer or musician dies, it can often be the main item in the bulletin. Some people might say its evening programmes are more important than its breakfast shows, but each one is presented, anchored or linked by a person who knows the subject intimately.

BBC Radio 4 is mainly speech based. Its morning show, *Today*, is one of the most listened-to speech-based programmes on either TV or radio in Britain. This is because, unlike in America, politicians and leaders of society here tend to favour the *Today* radio breakfast programme rather than breakfast television for their important interviews and announcements. Without wanting to detract from the programme's obvious attractions, the reasons for that are historical. Radio in this country was regarded as a national medium until the mid–1960s, so everything broadcast on Radio 4 tended to be of national interest – whereas in America, radio was essentially local. Also, until the 1980s there was no television at breakfast time in Britain. Anyway, back to Radio 4 – this channel carries a lot of news and news analysis, along with topical and current affairs programmes. It also broadcasts a fair number of dramas and serials (like *The Archers*), that are extremely highly regarded in the business. Radio 4 has programmes that usually last an hour or half an hour, and it has news bulletins 'on the hour'.

BBC Radio 5 Live is another speech channel, but concentrates on the 'laddish' cultural interests of sports mixed with topical opinion and news. The presenters talk about things you'd probably overhear being discussed at the bar over a drink! Radio 5 Live is the youngest of all the radio channels. It runs, very much like the popular music channels, on a day part basis and the presenters of the sequences tend to be like journalistic disc jockeys!

BBC Radio 6 (www.bbc.co.uk/6music) is an entirely web-based music radio station. It was launched on 11 March 2002 and centres around pop and rock music. Radio 6 also aims to promote some of the best up-and-coming music talent. The line-up of presenters includes musicians, journalists, comedians and broadcasters, so it has quite an eclectic theme and music value. It boasts strong editorial opinions and music news.

6 Music launched with the aim of setting the tone for the way radio is listened to and interacted with in a digital world. As well as the ability to listen online, 6 Music offers chatrooms run by presenters, message boards, live chats with guest bands and artists, email and SMS chat with the 6 Music team. What may be of particular interest to you is the web-cam view of life in the studio; you can tune into it via their web site and watch as a show goes on air: a great way to get a peek at a fully operational radio studio.

BBC Digital Radio also runs the Asian Network (which is exactly what it says), Radio 1xtra (new black music), Radio 7 (speech with comedy classics, kids programmes and drama), Five Live Sports Extra (yet more sport!) and the World Service, which is also broadcast on short wave throughout the world.

BBC Local Radio

The BBC started its local radio system in 1967 with the intention of creating a sort of 'mini-Radio 4' in each of the areas it served. In fact, the end product turned out to be more of a cross between Radio 2 and Radio 5, with music and speech in equal measure. Each station has developed its own character – Radio Merseyside would not sit comfortably in the shoes of, say, Radio Oxford, and Radio Newcastle would sound very different to Radio Bristol. These stations have done well to create, draw on and develop local talent. Local greengrocers have become football commentators, doctors have become chat show hosts, and shipyard workers have become disc jockeys. They have done well to re-create the old 'parish pump' atmosphere – the village water source where people met every day and swapped their news and gossip. There are 38 local stations in England, and more which broadcast to the national regions of Ireland, Scotland and Wales. If there is one near you, it is an excellent place to begin your broadcasting career, and for many people local radio happily spans the whole of their career. Each of the stations has a team of producers and presenters and a newsroom, which, besides feeding the local airwaves, also services national radio and sometimes television as well. People often progress into national radio and television from the local stations, so jobs are available quite frequently.

Commercial Radio

It would be pointless for me to go through the activities of each individual commercial station in the UK. They all have differences, but most sound remarkably similar if you're travelling from one end of the country to the other in your car! They all deliver a local service of information and news in between the fairly limited playlist of music that they specialize in. Most local stations can be described as 'hit radio', playing the Top 40 sounds of the day. There are a number of variations on the theme, but most play popular music.

The Standard Local Commercial Station

Most local radio stations earn the majority of their money between 7 a.m. and 9 a.m. each day. Without the income generated by advertising on the Breakfast Show the stations would be difficult to run. The rest of the day is divided similarly to BBC Radios 1 and 2, as described earlier. The next most important show on the station is the 'drivetime' show, which airs between 4 p.m. and 7 p.m. when a large number of listeners are on their way home from work. Listen to most of the stations for any length of time and you can determine a 'station sound'. Some stations have this station sound written down along with programme formats and style guides for all to adhere to; this is known as **house style**.

Often the presenters will sound very alike and their verbal references will be very similar. A lot of speech time on commercial radio is very restricted – sometimes as little as four minutes in an hour – which makes it difficult for the presenter's personality to shine through! However, it does make you work hard at getting your message and thoughts across very quickly and succinctly, which is good discipline. Quite a lot of stations are marketing themselves under a banner like: 'You're never more than 30 seconds away from a hit song' or they run two songs in a row together without interruption. This is known as a **segue** – songs played one after another without interruption, often with some attempt to blend the two musically together. A **sweep** of tunes is a number of tunes played back-to-back with no DJ interruption. Some station sweeps include station idents, but there is not much to be heard from the DJ. An audio item such as a jingle or station ident used as a piece of music is starting or finishing is known as a **drop-in**. It sounds very automatic, and so it is, a lot of it … but remember, there nearly always has to be someone there 'driving' the programme.

Most local stations run tight newsrooms, which supply news and information to programmes throughout the day. Some smaller stations close their newsrooms and hand over to a network news service as dusk approaches, but the need for people to supply information is always there. Other areas that make a station local are a good traffic and weather reporting system. And many stations also run a community-orientated 'What's On' diary.

Classic FM

A radio station that launched in September 1992 and proved that classical music doesn't have to be boring: it regularly hauls in over 5 million listeners. Classic is the only national commercial radio station on FM (which gives better quality reception than AM), and many of the more Top 40 proponents got very angry when the precious licence was awarded to a classical station.

It confounded its critics, however, largely due to the unfusty way the programmes are presented and the clear message that classical music can be enjoyed by all ages and a wide range of different people. The station has become something of a flagship for commercial radio.

Speech Radio

LBC (London Broadcasting Company) was launched in 1972, the first commercial station in the country. It changed its ownership and its name several times until 1996, when it finally settled down with a loyal audience. LBC started out with two frequencies (FM and AM), as did many of the original commercial stations, until the Radio Authority started a 'use it or lose it' campaign. The two frequencies split and one became the standard LBC talk and phone-in show (similar in format to Five Live); the other became a rolling news service provided by ITN. The station changed hands again in late 2002 and is now owned by the Chrysalis group.

Talk Radio, a national, independent station, went through similar problems and has ended up as an output to BBC Five Live and is now called TalkSport. One big asset in TalkSport's favour is its charismatic boss, Kelvin MacKenzie. Kelvin was the celebrated editor of Britain's most successful national daily newspaper, the *Sun*, until he left in the mid 1990s after around 15 years at the helm. He flirted, briefly, with running the satellite television system Sky, owned by the *Sun*'s proprietor Rupert Murdoch, before he bought the ailing Talk Radio station. He has made this national station the flagship of his burgeoning company, The Wireless Group.

The problem with speech radio is that it is labour intensive and thus expensive to run, which doesn't attract commercial operators one bit! It is also regarded by many as minority programming. To maximize its audience potential it has to provide an intelligent editorial approach whilst maintaining popularity with chat-based shows. If talk radio fails to include both ends of listener interest, its ratings drop and advertizers move away, so it ends up with no financing.

The Prospects

If you are good then you can achieve an above average standard of living, and there is the opportunity to augment your standard wage with anything from shop openings and feature writing for newspapers and magazines, to voice-over work. There is also the possibility of moving from radio to TV presenting à la Chris Tarrant of Capital FM and ITV's *Who Wants To Be A Millionaire*.

Those personalities earning really big bucks in radio, though, are few and far between; they are most likely to be TV personalities who make appearances on radio. In general radio is not so lucrative as TV. I would not advise anyone to enter into working in radio only for the money. Only when you reach the top of your field will you find that the money gets interesting. In contrast to TV, radio programmes can be made on a shoestring budget. The research, production, technical operating and performance of a radio show can be done by only one or two people. On several small local radio stations, due to tight budgets, a programme will be run by one person. In Britain radio is not always as attractive to advertizers as TV, so it does not pull in the revenue. In the US, however, radio manages to give TV a serious run for its money, and Britain is beginning to catch up.

MIKE'S WISE WORDS – 9

In radio you should only ever imagine that you are broadcasting to one person. Yes, I know there are millions of them out there, but each one listens to you personally and, sort of, imagines that you are talking directly to them. Never, never use the word 'you' in its plural sense – 'All of you out there' or 'Lots of you have written to me'. There's only one 'me' and this me hasn't written to anyone, yet. If you have to refer to groups, you should always use a word like 'people' or 'listeners'. 'I know a lot of people listening get really angry when ...' or 'Lots of listeners have written to me'. You are one person ... and he or she is your personal listener.

Work Experience

One of the ways to get experience in radio broadcasting, before you put your hand to the real thing, is to try your local hospital broadcasting system. Most hospital broadcasters have an over-18s policy, but it is usually possible to gain some sort of experience before you reach 18, taking requests and running errands – a great opportunity for the young enthusiast. All hospital radio operates on a volunteer basis and competition can be fierce, but if approached in the right way it can prove invaluable experience. It must be remembered, however, that hospital radio is there for the benefit of the sick; a hospital radio worker should have personal skills that allow them to behave sympathetically and with understanding to their listeners.

To get involved in hospital radio, contact your local hospital and they will put you through to the radio station if they have one. You are probably best trying on an evening or at weekends, when most stations are on air. You will probably be invited into the radio station to have a look around and a chat. If you want to go ahead and get involved you will probably be given a training programme or be attached to a programme to learn the ropes. At some stations you may need to go through an application procedure, which may involve the taking up of references. This is becoming more common, and is usually done for the hospitals' benefit for reasons of security and insurance.

The Low-Down on Hospital Radio

Over 90 per cent of the UK's hospital population has the benefit of hospital broadcasting. This means that over 18 million people can hear specially produced local hospital programmes every year. The benefits of hospital broadcasting services to both patients and staff are well recognized by the Department of Health. Stations are generally staffed entirely by volunteers and most are registered charities. The programmes are carefully produced to reflect the needs of the audience. They ensure that the patient is kept in touch with their local community, family and friends in a way no other broadcasting medium can. Some hospital stations are now on-air 24 hours a day.

Most hospitals are equipped with BBC and ILR radio and patients have the choice of several programmes throughout the day. Hospital broadcasting acts as an **opt-out** to one of these programmes and puts out over the hospital network an interesting programme, usually at a time of day when there is little medical activity and no visiting. Music often forms the basis of these programmes and careful selection of the musical items is a very important part of the broadcasters' work. Audience participation is a valuable asset in the therapeutic side of hospital broadcasting, so getting the patients to choose pieces of music to be played in the programme is a means of taking the patients' minds off themselves and onto the choice of records. Many hospital broadcasting stations also provide coverage of local sporting events in their area – another great way to get experience for bigger things.

You do not have to present programmes: there are other jobs going if you want to get involved. Most hospital radio stations are more than willing to find you something you are happy doing. You could be a ward-visitor (the most important job at most hospital radio stations), studio technician (the person who presses lots of buttons and gets no credit), fundraiser (the people who help the hospital radio stay alive), or news/sports researcher (fancy title for someone who gets the latest soccer results and news bulletins).

Student Radio

If you are still studying, here is an excellent way of looking at the prospects in broadcasting. Campus radio offers opportunities to many students to check out exactly what goes into making a radio show, and allows students to have a go at virtually every job available in radio. Every large college and university that offers media courses has a campus radio station, and although you may not be promised the widest of audiences, it offers a great opportunity to get to grips with radio.

Most student radio stations are members of the Student Radio Association, the national representative body of the medium in the UK. The SRA, which is affiliated to the Radio Academy, offers member stations national representation, a range of support and training services, a communications network and regular conferences. Many stations are also subscribed to the Student Broadcast Network, a syndicated sustaining service that offers a range of advertizing and overnight programming for subscribing stations.

Student radio in the UK is over 30 years old, with about 80 student radio groups active across the country. Student radio stations perform a number of functions at the universities and colleges where they are based – they offer a radio service geared specifically to the student and youth population in the local area, they offer students interested in pursuing a career in broadcasting an opportunity to get hands-on experience and, often, they offer a cutting-edge style of music and programming greatly lacking from mainstream commercial radio.

Jobs and Experience in Student Radio

Different student stations broadcast in different ways. Current broadcasting techniques include:

- RSL Broadcasting: Stations which broadcast for (up to) 28 days at a time across a city or town on a FM frequency. Licence restrictions mean these stations can only do two RSL broadcasts per year (one in London).

- LPAM Broadcasting: Stations which broadcast full time on AM, but are restricted to a specific campus.
- Induction Loop Broadcasting: Stations which broadcast full time on AM to anyone living within a specific 'loop' of cable, normally a given campus.
- PA / Hard-wire Broadcasting: Stations which broadcast at specific times over a PA system to halls of residence or similar buildings.

Internet Broadcasting

Many stations broadcast on the web, normally in addition to other broadcasting methods, although in a number of cases they are stand-alone internet stations.

US Radio Stations

Radio in the US is great! You don't have to stick to the UK to gain experience – you can learn abroad or take a gap year and spend it in the US, learning some new ideas and techniques to take home . . .

Stations in the US use call letters instead of names. Call letters usually comprise of three or four letters. Those stations beginning with a 'W' tend to be east of the Mississippi River. Those beginning with a 'K' tend to be west of the river. Sometimes names are added on the end. WFXF is also known as The Fox: 'WFXF The Fox'.

So What Do We Know Now?

- *Radio is a more flexible medium than television*
- *It's a good place to start your broadcasting career*
- *Radio is expanding more than ever before, thanks to satellite and digital developments*
- *Hospital radio and student radio stations are excellent for gaining experience*
- *Music radio is dominant but speech radio is still doing well*

CHAPTER 4

New media

So What is New Media?

New media is the general term given to the constantly changing way in which entertainment and information is being delivered to consumers. In many ways it is a moving target but, at present, it encompasses the Internet, WAP phones, **digital** *television and set top boxes, as opposed to our traditional means of communicating like newspapers,* **analogue** *television, books and analogue radio (sometimes known as* **old media***). In recent years the emergence of email and the Internet in the home as well as at work means that new media has come to play an ever-increasing part in our lives. One of the more respected practitioners in the business has described it to me as 'Everything that isn't old media – it includes the digital developments and interactive television. Anywhere where the user has control over the content and it is delivered in digital format.'*

Where is it Taking Us?

In the early days of the new millennium, the buzzwords around the broadcasting business were **digital**, **broadband**, **interactivity** and **convergence**. What was happening was that all the forms of electronic communications known to us were switching to use a similar form of transmission – a digital system where the signal was divided into binary units, similar to computer language. Britain led the world in switching its mobile phone system to digital. Its television and radio transmissions followed quickly, as did its music and video systems (CD and DVD were digital), computers were already based on a digital system and now our landline telephones were switching over as well, with high-speed **ADSL** and **ISDN** links.

Suddenly, all the forms of electronic media were able to talk to each other. Theoretically to begin with, but now more and more in practice, you could use the same equipment to address the Internet, watch a DVD, listen to a CD, watch television, listen to radio, text to mobile phones, and place audio and video phone calls. This coming together of all the technologies was labelled **convergence**.

Convergence is bringing more overlap among print, TV, radio and web journalism. It became possible to be, say, a DJ performing with CDs on the radio in London, being heard via the Internet in Los Angeles, being texted by someone from Hong Kong and being phoned on a mobile phone from Sydney. And, for good measure, the world could probably watch you in the studio via a web cam. A person may work in two or three separate media in a single shift. The same interaction was true of all forms of electronic media – suddenly the desktop, laptop or handheld PC/mobile phone became a major information and entertainment exchange.

Moving pictures also became possible on the Internet and were improved by high-speed links – so what was a one-hour *Big Brother* programme on Channel 4, became a 24-hour broadband experience via the *Big Brother* web site. And you could use the same equipment you were watching on to vote who should be thrown out of the house next, or to read more about the inmates.

It doesn't take much imagination to see how, with new media encompassing all these different forms of entertainment and infor-mation, the number of jobs needing to be done has also increased.

MIKE'S WISE WORDS – 10

Beware of going into a job interview in traditional media such as TV, radio or newspapers and calling them 'old media'. That's not the way they like to think of themselves, as they struggle to keep up with all the developments that technology can throw at them. The term 'old media' is best left to show how upbeat and trendy you are when in a new media only situation.

Communications Systems

In a way we are experiencing a second industrial revolution, with the development of the information society. Mobile phones, email, the Internet, cable TV, personal computers, all the wonders of the information society, are increasingly a common part of everyday life.

Telecommunications companies are changing the way we function in our everyday lives, and changing it forever. As we move towards this information-based society, easy and affordable universal access to telecom services will be crucial to find jobs, enjoy leisure, receive and send information, practise citizenship and ensure democracy.

Using New Media

So we have a new period of media development, one that gets to grips with the significance of new communications technologies in our world. It is a development that everyone can learn about and put into practice: old or young, technophobe or PC whiz-kid. It is not just a form of information technology but an accessible social and cultural application; a place, for instance, where we can see viewing schedules for TV channels and book seats for the theatre.

By the end of the twentieth century, the various existing branches of media could be said to have begun to lose their way. The arrival of the web changed a large number of previously held conceptions, including the way audiences, readers and individuals use the media. The people in control of the media – editors, programme controllers – who dictated the way in which we would receive our information and entertainment suddenly found that, instead, we could make our own decisions. The web foreshadowed a world in which we could access the material of our own choice, when we wanted it, and no longer be at the mercy of a scheduler. There has had to be a complete rethink of the way broadcasters address audiences and the ways we can measure the number of people watching or listening.

Computers and New Media

People turn to television, radio and their web sites for news and information. And this won't change. Whether the economy is good or bad, news will be in demand – a vital element of our daily lives. Journalists fill that demand and they are beginning to use and exploit all the facilities that our information society supplies. Moving from print to electronic media is not uncommon; it is now advisable that TV personnel should have the know-how to combine their activities with a knowledge of the web and its applications.

Technology beams instant television, radio and web reports from anywhere in the world. As cable, the web and related technologies grow, so do the sources – the kinds of information available and their application to the broadcasting industry. The mass media is a growth industry in services and careers, so it is absolutely necessary to learn to use a computer effectively for word processing, retrieving information, using the Internet and web page construction.

The web is a treasure-house of knowledge; good knowledge of the web gives you the ability to do people favours – older guys in TV and radio stations are more likely to get lost wandering around the web and confused when their PC packs up … If you can step in there to help, you will gain respect from your bosses.

MIKE'S WISE WORDS – 11

The Internet (see below – the web and the Internet are different!) has begun to lose its reputation as being full of computer geeks swapping episode guides to *Star Trek*. The student who spent all day, every day, stumbling around the Net in his college computer room is now a relic of the past. The early days used to be like someone wandering around a museum, gazing curiously at the cases but with no idea about how to identify and research what he or she saw. Now, with IT-based education and an opening up of the web to the masses, thanks to those good people running Yahoo, Google and Ask Jeeves it is amazingly easy to access any information you require, with a high speed link, in a matter of seconds.

The Internet and the Web

To avoid any confusion, let's clarify a few points about the world wide web (www) and the Internet. If you think of a traditional net and put a spider's web across each of the holes of the net, that gives you an idea of what we are looking at. The web runs on the Internet. The Internet is the name for a global network of computers, interconnected together to access and exchange information. Rumours that it started life as a sinister US military experiment may be slightly exaggerated, although a computer network run by the US Defense Department in the latter half of the twentieth century did lay the foundations for the system we now have.

It's difficult to pinpoint the Internet. It is a mass of cables, wires and microprocessors, which carry any kind of data such as computer programmes and email facilities. Every computer has the ability to be a server to the web when it is connected. You can see this if you link to a web exchange site like Kazaa – people can take information from you even as you are downloading stuff from the web.

The first event in the life of the Internet as we know it today came in 1974. Information could be put into a 'packet' and addressed so that computers on the network would pass it along, in the right direction, until it arrived at its destination. Various tests and demonstrations were successfully conducted, and internet-style networks started to take off. However it was 10 years before the **TCP/IP**-based Internet rolled out across the USA in 1983. And even then it remained primarily the domain of academics and scientists for another 10 years before breaking out and overtaking the public sector.

How the Web is Different

The web is, in effect, the 'shop window' of the Internet. The dream behind the web is of a common information space in which we communicate by sharing information. It is the modern equivalent of the market place or parish-pump. Its universality is essential: the fact that a **hypertext** link can point to anything, be it personal, local or global, be it draft or highly polished.

The web is simpler than much of the Internet, in that it runs on a single language format: HyperText Markup Language (**HTML**). This is a simple, easy to use, universally readable computer language carried by the Internet and used to create web pages.

The Web and Business

The web is arguably the most powerful business tool in human history. It is useless, however, in the absence of sound business principles and an understanding of how it works in relation to regular people. Nearly all TV and radio companies have begun to use the web to reach out to new audiences and to supply their existing audiences with the best service they can. The web saves time and allows us to access information at the touch of a button. Without leaving my chair, I can read up-to-the-minute news from all over the world. We now can keep in touch with contacts all over the world at no extra cost.

THE PROFESSIONAL'S VIEW – PAUL CAMPBELL

Paul Campbell, who has launched new media companies Bell Media and Liberty Bell after working as a television and radio producer at the BBC, has provided web site activity for many of the country's top television companies.

Although the companies have a strong concentration on providing web sites for programmes such as *This Morning* on ITV, Paul has also pioneered interactivity between television programmes and their audiences:

Interactive television has forced programme makers to listen to what the viewer wants. A few years ago the only interaction between programme makers and the audience at home was to conduct a phone-in. Now all programming is influenced by an associated web site. Audiences feel someone is taking notice of what they have to say and what they want.

For a newcomer to the business it's an exciting place to be and the job opportunities are enormous. It is easy to cross over into new media, to learn new skills and move around to jobs where you can apply them: I have taken on generally trained graduates and turned them into new media people with a small amount of training.

Working With The Web

Media and the web work well together because they are both about communicating and audiences. The web brings communicators together, building communities and displaying media products, texts or artworks to a global audience. Without the web many individuals and small groups would not have the resources to find an audience for their work. A web site can be your own magazine and gallery. Anything that can be put into words or pictures – or animation, video or music – can be put there. To people of an earlier generation (like me!) it's a fantastic liberator.

Introduction to Broadband

There are many companies offering broadband Internet services in the UK. There is no single definition of 'broadband'. It basically means a faster than standard internet connection. Also, it is 'always on', so once your computer is switched on the connection is always immediately available. The speed of data over an internet connection is measured in thousands of bits (kilobits) per second – kbit/s. Broadband data rates are typically ten times faster than a telephone dial-up modem.

The higher speed is appealing, but the fact that it's always on can be just as valuable. People often find they use the Internet in a completely new way once they are freed from the worry of mounting phone bills or missing a vital call. Email and instant messaging programmes can be left running so you can keep in touch continuously.

Broadband Internet can be used to deliver video. However, to deliver full-screen broadcast quality TV would need a connection speed of 2 mbit/s or more – over four times faster than most current services to the home. Despite this, compared to using a dial-up telephone modem, video delivered by broadband is much better looking, smoother and doesn't suffer from **buffering** problems.

File uploads and downloads are much faster. You can easily download large documents and files, such as multimedia presentations or computer software. All this means that TV shows and movies will be available through the Internet from all over the world. At present real-time downloading is not really possible with domestic high-speed links. Movies can be downloaded with an ADSL link, but it takes anything between four and eight hours for a standard 90-minute film. But as the links become faster and the software is developed, it will be possible to view as you download and then either wipe it or transfer to DVD from the hard drive. No longer will we in Britain have to wait for the new series of *Friends* or *Frasier*: we will be able to order it off the Internet in advance.

ADSL

This is a technology to 'supercharge' a standard phone line so that it can carry data signals at the same time as normal phone calls. ADSL allows the real-time download of video clips and makes sending large files such as photographs quicker.

Cable

Cable TV companies are able to use their networks to deliver Internet data as well as TV programmes. Some digital cable TV boxes already have a cable modem built in, but these are only available in digital cable coverage areas.

Broadband Wireless

A connection via a low-power microwave radio link. The company will install an outside antenna, about the size of a small satellite dish, and a small indoor unit that connects to your computer. The antenna points at their base-station transmitter located on a high building nearby.

Webcasting

As well as carrying its own material, the web can also be used for carrying the digital signals of traditional broadcasting. **Webcasting** is growing as people subscribe to broadband Internet connections. Radio stations are now multiplying on the net – some Internet-only and some feeding the output of local stations to a wider audience. Television pictures can be **streamed** live over the net and the usage is growing. The change to digital transmission in broadcasting only helps to speed this process.

One web company, which sadly recently folded, was putting out five channels (it called them **vortals** – or video **portals**) daily of information and entertainment on a 24-hour basis. Elsewhere, you can access libraries of recorded material, such as video clips etc., and it is rapidly becoming possible to **download** complete programmes to your home computer. Think of the future if this development continues. You might eventually get all your programmes direct from the makers, on subscription, without ever having to go through a broadcaster or an aerial! And that's another thing to think about when you go for an interview for a job in the broadcast business.

New Media and Digital

The UK is widely viewed as a global leader for the development and usage of new technologies. At the time of writing, 10 million of the 24 million homes in the UK have interactive services, representing 40 per cent of the market. Heavy investments and commitments by the BBC and Rupert Murdoch's Sky satellite service have helped to introduce a new kind of television and radio to the UK. People currently have a unique relationship with television and radio. They tend to place more trust in broadcasting than they do in the web; TV has always been there, we've all grown up with it, it's part of all our lives and it's status is that much higher and more central to us. As a result of this unique relationship, interacting with programmes is more appealing and compelling than interacting with even the user-friendly web sites.

In the future a form of immersive TV will almost certainly be invented, to give a feeling that you are really there using a wide field of view, allowing the picture to surround you. Electronic programme guides will help you to set up your own viewing schedule, etc.

MIKE'S WISE WORDS – 12

With the digital revolution, there has come a whole host of new **generic** channels. Unfortunately all these new channels do not mean lots more jobs, especially for newcomers to the business. In the case of such channels as UK Gold, Bravo, Granada Plus and TNT Cartoon Network, a lot of the shows have all been made and are simply being repeated. The main function of these generic channels is to provide the platform for a library of material. There are jobs, but they are mainly in the **presentation** area. Some children's channels make quite a bit out of linking two programmes together – they have phone-in requests and people play small competitions between shows. Often the **links** for these programmes are all recorded in one day of activity in the studio, each week.

Digital TV and Radio

Digital television is expanding rapidly. It has already been taken up by about a third of the population and offers the potential to access over 200 channels and other services, including interactive television and the Internet. The government expects all television transmissions to be digital between 2006 and 2010. There are also teletext services available through both BBC and commercial TV, which carry news, sport, travel, weather and other information, and also offer subtitling – making viewing and access to material on the TV easier both for deaf people and for foreign-language speakers.

It is a time of exciting developments in broadcasting and each of the new viewing possibilities and interactive facilities will need people with varied skills and a fresh new outlook on broadcasting and what should be expected of it. If you want to access a career in broadcasting it is absolutely essential that you have a firm grip on what the implications of the digital revolution are for the communications system. Where long ago the TV set made its way into the homes of the general public and, shock horror, spoke to them, told them stories and showed them pictures, now TV is taking on an entirely different role in people's lives. Now the television set is seen as a means of communicating, of viewing, of organizing. It is part of society in the home and in the public sectors, and it will only become more established in the future.

Interactive TV

It is possible to interact with the digital TV in your home. The digital signals, whether from land-based transmitters or satellites, are decoded through the set top box (STB). Using the STB it is possible now to 'talk back' to the broadcaster. You can compete in game shows and purchase products advertised on TV by pressing interactive buttons. It is even possible to direct your own viewing by selecting different camera angles during a broadcast sports match.

I've talked about the *Big Brother* interactivity. The BBC's *East-Enders* 'soap opera' is another interactive show; it has a web site linked through the BBC's main web site. When the *EastEnders* homepage comes up there is a section for leaving messages discussing your thoughts on the characters. There is somewhere you can sub-scribe to the web site newsletter; there is a web cam you can click onto to check out what's happening in the Square – day or night, filming or no filming. You can choose to go for a tour round the Square and its adjoining streets. There are updates on the happenings; there are actor interviews. You can check out a backstage map of the sets and go for a virtual tour. And finally there are games and quizzes with prizes to be won. This all serves to bring the viewer closer to the show and allows them to interact with the actors, writers, producers and other viewers.

MIKE'S WISE WORDS – 13

Do you know why programmes like *EastEnders* are called soap operas? It's because in the USA, the daily serials that used to go out on television were so popular that they become the major targets for advertising. The biggest commercial battleground at the time was between washing powder companies anxious to advertise their wares to the buying public. In order to keep out their rivals, these soap companies started to produce their own daily serials to sell to the TV networks, with the proviso that only their brand of soap powder could be advertised in the breaks. These sponsored serials thus got the nickname 'soap operas'.

Consumers are showing interest in the ability to interact with extra entertainment content (such as with shows like *Jeopardy* and *Who Wants To Be A Millionaire*) and other viewers. These applications may not create new revenue streams, but they may divert attention from the advertisements.

Why Learn About Interactive TV?

Millions of homes in the UK have access to interactive TV over satellite, cable and terrestrial broadcast services. Commercial information television operations in the US have had widespread success. One day the television, computer and telephone may converge for video, data and voice services on an Internet that's everywhere.

Interactive (digital) television is most easily understood as the convergence of Internet-like interactivity and traditional television programming and delivery technology. Making TV interactive involves the addition of responsive, user-controlled elements to traditional broadcast video and audio signals. Simply put, this means that the Internet, with its web sites and chat room facilities, is combined with traditional TV sets, and programme makers devise programmes which use all the facilities of the Internet.

Many interactive services do not require a return path connection from the receiver back to the service provider. Additional information on programmes, different camera views, games and enhanced teletext services are normally broadcast with the programmes and are selected by the viewer using their digital receiver. To access the Internet and send emails a telephone modem connection is needed.

The Digital Interactive Television Group (DITG) is a firm that offers a package of services to companies setting up interactive channels, including software, studio and production facilities and digital expertise. Digital interactive television is everything the Internet wanted to be. It is a simplistic and trusted medium that is in 10 million homes in the UK and has huge potential to generate revenues. So far it has been misunderstood. Real interactivity is not just about flicking through to Sky Sports Active or BBCi, it's about viewers genuinely interacting with the content.

Interactive TV for the Future

Revenues can be made through interactive television, perhaps most obviously through games and gaming. Video games can be pay-per-play, and casino-style gambling or bingo can also be charged for as well as offering the temptation of cash prizes. Large commercial brands will also be able to start up their own TV channels, such as football clubs and DIY stores (running almost constant adverts for tools and decorating ideas ...) and, of course, shopping malls which include many different stores. It has been estimated that such channels could be set up for as little as £1 million per year, which is not even a dent in big corporations' yearly advertising budgets.

Interactive Sports

By far and away the most popular interactive services are for sports. People get into sport very quickly, partly because they seem to have a level of interest in sport that verges on passion. There are a variety of applications that people can use, like 'player cam', where you can focus on your favourite player; changing camera angles, etc. to get the most out of the match; instant access to statistics; and multiple broadcast streams, different versions of the same game being transmitted simultaneously.

A New Remote?

I believe that very soon the remote control will be replaced with a mobile phone-style handset, enabling people to send text messages to their TV using a familiar format. The text messages will work either to communicate with the programme maker or to use a recording or pausing facility on their STB. MTV and Nickelodeon have had a lot of success with encouraging their viewers to use their mobile phones to interact with their programming. Viewers can vote for the programme they wish to view next. At the moment all viewers have to watch the most popular choice of programme, but I anticipate that, sometime soon, you'll be able to demand to view one of the, say, three programmes offered. If there is more than one STB in a household, two people could be watching entirely different programmes on the same channel in the same house.

Another benefit of using a mobile phone is the ability to participate with a programme whilst watching it with other people who do not wish to participate, thus not interfering with their viewing experience. Some programmes are now offering downloads for mobile phones to make interactivity even easier, and it's another way for programmes to extend their brands. By adding a computer-like device to the television set and providing a communication path back to the broadcaster, the viewer can be invited to interact with the programming, enjoy some level of control over the experience and provide feedback. This closes the loop between TV content creators, TV content distributors, advertisers, merchants and viewers. Viewers can speak directly to the TV content creators.

Text Messaging

Of all the new technologies to emerge over the past decade, none has achieved such immediacy of take-up as SMS. Although it has been 10 years since the first **SMS** – or text message – was sent over Vodafone's UK network, the phenomenal growth of **texting** has happened in a much shorter time, growing from virtually nothing to more than 45 million text messages per day in less than four years. However, it's only recently that media owners have started to use SMS interactivity to forge deeper relationships with users and advertisers.

Although each company is using different models, what is driving the move towards SMS interactivity is the knowledge that mobile marketing can not only increase brand loyalty, but also provide a substantial cash flow in itself. Through initiatives such as reverse billing, mobile marketers get to have their cake and eat it, capturing vital data from users, readers and listeners and grabbing a slice of SMS tariffs at the same time.

The Beeb and New Media

The BBC is a **public service broadcaster**, perhaps more readily associated with old media, communicating with millions of licence fee payers. It is also the home of the largest web site in Europe and a pioneer of interactive television and home storage. The New Media division is designed to look not only at the opportunities of the present but at those of the future as well. TV companies are beginning to realize that innovation, creativity, agility, consumer focus and collaboration are the key to new media's success.

The New Media division includes BBC Online, Interactive Television and Navigation and **Imagineering**. BBC Online has become the UK's most popular web site, with over 190 million page impression requests per month. The site is organized into popular categories like Kids, Entertainment and Sport. Imagineering is all about capturing the content of the future and giving the opportunity to bring interactive ideas to life.

BBCi

BBCi is the new media wing of the BBC. The 'i' stands for interactive, and it takes in computers, mobile phones and personal organizers, and interactive digital television across Sky, ITV Digital and the cable companies. This approach is both desirable and necessary in an age when we want our content wherever we are. BBCi is the interactive, information-based web site for BBC viewers. It has links to all the web sites of its best shows: *EastEnders*, *Top of the Pops*, etc. You can find out what's on the BBC, and about your local news and weather. It's a very exciting area – it's new, young and cool!

What Sort of Person Works in New Media?

A number of people are finding that their skills learned at college, or just at home, are transferable into the world of new media. If you are computer literate, understand HTML, writing and graphic layout, and broadcasting – in pictures or words – all of these are relevant in working on the net.

Because it's such a new area, you may not be able to show particular qualifications, but what you can do when you apply for jobs in this sector is to build up a portfolio of examples of your work. Print out web pages that you have been involved in, download video and audio work that you have prepared – it's all the equivalent of the 'press cuttings album' of yesterday.

Radio and television journalists are at the heart of it all, assisting technology as it beams instant television, radio and web reports from anywhere in the world. As the cable, web and related technologies grow, so do the sources and kinds of information available. The mass media is a growth industry in services – and careers.

Above all, you'll need to demonstrate an open mind and a keenness to innovate, which should be no problem, especially if you're young.

So What Do We Know Now?

- *New media covers digital developments in communications, including the web, mobile phones, digital TV and radio*
- *Jobs in new media are plentiful and could be easier to get than those in old media*
- *Broadband transmission could lead to more people watching television on their home computers*
- *Web-only radio and TV stations are on the increase*
- *Interactive TV and radio is affecting the way we use old media*

Radio and Television Presenting

CHAPTER 5

General Presenting and Using an Agent

The Final Link in the Chain

Presenting is the final link in the broadcast chain. Yours is the last voice on air. So if someone in the production team has come up with an idea for a story and guest to interview, they would write a brief for you, giving you the main points of the story, what the guest is likely to say, etc., and then you are the person to convey effectively that story to the listener/viewer by asking, hopefully, the right questions – the sort of questions that the public would want answered, and so on. What you need to do is study the way various people present their shows, from the news to the pop show, from an animal hospital programme to a makeover show, and so on. Think about the presenters you have seen and what they do. Of course, different programmes use presenters in different ways (and there's also a trend away from having a presenter at all on some sorts of shows), but some things are common to all.

Jumping Ahead?

You do know this is the middle of the book, don't you? I'm just checking . . . just in case you're one of those people who is absolutely burning to be a TV or radio presenter and nothing else, and that's why you've ended up straight here!

I get a lot of people who come storming through my door, telling me that they want to be a presenter. When I suggest that maybe they should consider starting at the bottom and working up, work behind the scenes for a while to get to know the ropes, a fair proportion just glaze over. As far as they're concerned the job in front of the camera or microphone is the only one – and no other substitutes will be accepted.

At least they're being honest, and they do possess the one thing that'll help propel them to the top – arrogance, or supreme self-confidence. However, I don't think I can remember one person who knocked my door down in that way and refused all other suggestions, and then did make it right to the top. Unless you count Chris Evans, but that's another story ...

Try reading from the front of the book if you can. There's a lot of good advice there. But if you did turn straight here first and won't turn back, then good luck, and read on.

A Lucky Break?

It is estimated that only 20 per cent of production and 5 per cent of presentation jobs are advertised. Unfortunately, even when a job is advertised it is far more likely that this had been done for reasons of legality or some internal politics and the successful candidate has already been chosen. Harsh reality though this is, don't let it completely depress you. There are many examples of people who were completely unknown before they suddenly appeared on our screens, and many who hadn't even been in a studio before they were picked to present a programme. You can do it too but never forget – don't underestimate the obstacles that will be placed in your way.

Presenting Qualities

I've got to say it: some presenters are pretty insufferable people, because of the very quality they need to do the job – they need to be supremely self-centred. Of course, a lot of other things follow that. First, you have got to be fairly presentable – not dramatically good looking but someone who won't frighten the horses at least. And you've got to know how to look after yourself, the sort of person who wouldn't be alone for long at parties and other gatherings. Then you have to be overwhelmingly self-confident. Shy and retiring need not apply. Arrogance can be good for this job, but not so arrogant that you can't/won't listen to someone else. Whilst it helps if you're a show-off, it's not always the loudest person in the bar who makes the best presenter. Sometimes the quietest of people come to life in front of a camera or microphone.

You will be a natural communicator, or at least someone who can put together good scripts that convey points simply and under-standably.

MIKE'S WISE WORDS – 14

What you must do, especially in television, is fully understand that several other people are involved in your performance: director, producer, music librarian, cameraperson, etc. Sir David Frost, the chat show host and presenter, has always been known as an affable, friendly but highly professional person in the studio. One of his greatest attributes is that he never seems to forget other people and their names, and that's a great gift in itself. But also, in the studio David is courteous and friendly to the studio crew. He's known for his catchphrase 'Hello, Good Morning and Welcome', but he never forgets to say 'Hello', 'Thank you' and 'Goodbye' behind the scenes as well. It's important. If the studio crew think you value them, they'll look after you. If not, well . . . I have known some potentially brilliant careers overshadowed by poor lighting, badly framed pictures and a face that looks like a lost sheep!

An ability to memorize and recall facts, figures and storylines is invaluable, but there are tricks you can learn to help you on your way. On radio, the time to speak is often quite limited (sometimes down to four minutes an hour on music radio). So think about what you're going to say and write it down. Make sure it sounds good before you open your mouth.

On television the use of autocue has developed to a good extent, but it won't always be there, so you need to have other ways of knowing what you're going to say. In news circles, where the 'piece to camera' or **PTC** is part of the stock in trade, some people have developed the use of a mini-recorder on which they record their script. They then play it back through an invisible earpiece and simply repeat the words, a micro-second behind.

Another way to keep the whole thing spontaneous is to think about the piece you're about to do, isolate some key words and write those out on a piece of card that stays in your view. Each key word then triggers off a whole new set of thoughts and makes you look ingenious and spontaneous! It also avoids you sounding like you are reading off paper. But we're jumping ahead of ourselves.

Why Do You Want to Be a Presenter?

The straight answer for a lot of people is that the job looks fun and it makes you famous. But, frankly, that's not a good enough reason and it won't impress at the interview or audition stage. The BBC has done some surveys on what makes good presenters and they've come up with four categories – I'll tell you more about it later, but one thing is important: you need to tick more than one category to get in. The four are: Expert, Journalist, Wannabe, Celebrity. You can't just be a wannabe. You have to be at least one of the other three, preferably more.

And, yes it is fun to do, which is what can make it good to watch as well – but not if the whole thing is like an in-joke with your mates. It is actually hard work to get it right and make it look easy. The more professional you are about the job, the more relaxed you look, the better it comes over. And the viewer or listener isn't daft. If your enthusiasm for something is faked, it comes over in your voice and in your eyes.

So think about it carefully. Do you want it? Do you really want it? Or do you just want the things it brings with it?

THE PROFESSIONAL'S VIEW – ANNE DIAMOND

Anne Diamond, apart from being my ex-wife, is also a superb broadcaster and an example of how luck can play a big part in your career. Anne, the first major star of breakfast television in the UK, didn't originally want to be in television at all – she was keen on music and went into higher education to study the flute. Having reached a point where she didn't feel able to take her music further, she spotted a job as a music critic for a newspaper group in the West Country.

While she worked for the newspapers she also studied journalism at Cardiff, and eventually started general reporting. On one story she followed a group of handicapped local children to America and when she came back the local television station invited her in to talk about it. Hey presto! The TV boss was so impressed with her appearance that he offered her a job as a telly reporter. She climbed the ladder until, before she was 30, Anne was invited to replace the infamous 'Famous Five' at Britain's first breakfast television station, TV-am.

> If I had accepted the first knock-back I got, I could be still writing about music. Instead I looked for the opportunities of gaining experience in all sorts of programmes and I was always prepared to move house if a job was worth it. Be warned, though – the price of fame is a fairly bitchy rumour mill about your private life and what you did to get a job. Plenty of people want to offer you advice, but always

be true to yourself and follow your own instincts about where your next promotion might come.

Preparing

Start by watching the television or listening to the radio, especially the sort of programmes you would like to present. Really study all the shows that are fronted by presenters. Which type of programme do presenters work on? Which type of presenter fits which type of programme? How are these put together and how does the presenter fit in? Do they link items together or control the direction of the show? How is the programme *House Call* different to *DIY SOS*?

How do the presenters 'talk' to the camera or microphone? How do they dress? How do they speak? What do they have in common and how do some stand out? How do they take a boring topic and make it interesting and engaging? How do they cope with the unexpected?

The more TV and radio you analyse, the better idea you'll have of some of the key attributes you'll need, the different presenting styles and some of the problems.

Practice Makes Perfect

Although TV presenters differ from show to show, channel to channel, and station to station, they do share some common approaches and skills. The more of these you are aware of, and practise, the better your style will be and the greater chance you'll have of impressing!

MIKE'S WISE WORDS – 15

Chris Tarrant, the television presenter and radio DJ, tells of how he came home after an exhausting day in the studio presenting *Who Wants to Be a Millionaire?* His young son came up to him as he sank into his comfortable armchair and started to pull him out of it again. 'Not now,' said Chris, 'I've had a hard day.' His son looked at him, flabbergasted, and said, 'A hard day? All you do is sit in a chair and read out loud!' That's what you get, Chris, for making it look so easy!

Reading Out Loud

A way to develop this key skill is by reading a script aloud from a computer screen. The trick is to look like it's all coming off the top of your head while speaking smoothly. Make up your own piece – say, 45 seconds on your favourite TV show – and practise presenting it. Try to talk as if you are having a conversation. Think about the way your voice sounds, how your head moves and the way your eyes interact with the camera or microphone and your audience. Get your friends and family to listen to you and be ruthless in their criticism!

Learn to ad-lib freely. Try deviating from the script, unless you're practising reading the news – you are supposed to be communicating, not reading. This is a crucial skill when doing live TV or radio. What if the unexpected happens? What if the autocue breaks down in the middle of your link? You'll need to cope and make the link appear relaxed and seamless.

Don't develop an 'on air' voice – you know the dreadful way some people answer the phone or talk at you on the radio like a train announcer. Keep yourself relaxed. A way to practise this is to read a news item or something similar a few times out loud. After repeating it several times, get a friend to take the paper away and ask you to tell them about the story you've just been reading out. If, when you do this, your voice changes substantially, then you need to work on it so you end up 'telling' rather than 'reading'.

What Do You Look Like?

Even though I've been in the business quite a long time, I still find it difficult to tell how someone will look 'on camera'. Take a look at the on-screen you. Try to get hold of a camcorder and take at peek at what you look like. Don't be surprised if the lens shows a different image of you than you expected! Compare how you look and act on screen with other presenters. Start by just talking to the camera about yourself. Keep it to two minutes, and get a friend to give you hand signals every 30 seconds and count you down the last 10. Practise finishing cleanly and calmly on zero – you'll soon get to know how long 10 seconds really is! (Three words to a second, usually.) Make sure you bring your talk to a natural conclusion rather than stopping dead because you've run out of time. Presenters do this all the time, so it's a great technique to master. If the words dry up, just say what you're thinking. And have fun – it will come across. Try smiling (if it's appropriate) when you read something out – you can actually *hear* the smile!

MIKE'S WISE WORDS – 16

A checklist for you in your drive to be a presenter:

- The media business is all about communication. You have to be able to get on with people.

- Keep smiling, even if they change your script at the last minute.
- Listen to direction. If you don't understand, ask.
- Exude a confident, happy air at all times.
- When you are new stay out of everyone's way until you are needed.
- Learn your lines even if a prompting device is available.
- Try to be as fresh for the thirtieth take as you were for the first.
- Remember, there is no set career route.
- Recognize your level of experience and understand that you will have to work your way up.
- Be prepared to invest time, and perhaps money, in developing your skills and knowledge.

You are not alone! Thousands of young people want to be a presenter. If you thought *Popstars* was a competition from hell, then be prepared for more of the same. Making it as a TV or radio presenter can be equally as tough. But the broadcast landscape is changing. There are more and more TV and radio stations and programmes so the opportunities for presenters have never been better. And everyone is desperate to uncover the next big thing – the face and voice of the future.

Using An Agent
Remember that I am an agent, and you might, therefore, think that my thoughts on this subject are quite biased. However, I have held my views on agents for quite a long time, long before I became one myself. My time as an agent has only re-inforced the views that you are about to read.

Do I Need an Agent?
Agents are really only of use to those lucky few who actually get on screen or behind the microphone of a top radio show. Once you have spoken those first tentative words in the studio or on an OB (outside broadcast), you may decide it's time to get an agent; the information below should help you with that decision and help you to choose the one that is right for you. I must say again that agents are only useful for presenters and performers: producers and researchers have no need for agents and agents cannot really help them unless they wish to enter the presenting forum!

A lot of people in this business are just in love with the idea of being able to say 'Call my agent'. But you should think very carefully before you consider having an agent. To all new people who approach me, I ask, 'What is it that you think an agent will do?' Can an agent actually do something you can't do yourself? Are you sure you want to give someone 15 per cent of your earnings when you've already made a success of things yourself?

Think also about this: a successful agent has more than one person on their books. Say the average agent has 50 people; how long does that mean the agent spends each day thinking about you? And how long do *you* think about you each day? Exactly.

Does it sound like I've been trying to do myself out of a job? Well, not exactly. I'm just trying to make people be realistic about what an agent can and can't do. It's not the agent that gets you a job, it's you.

So What Does an Agent Do?

An agent is someone who represents you, and takes bookings on your behalf for a percentage of the fee. Agents are the gatekeepers to the people who hire you for radio, TV, film and commercials – the casting directors and producers. They should send out your new pictures and tapes to the right organizations and be on the ball when any new job presents itself. The advantage of having a good agent on your side is that they will have access to a lot of contacts and tend to know of auditions coming up which haven't been advertised. When there's a bite they can usually negotiate a higher rate and sort out all the contract work surrounding things like repeat fees.

What an agent does is to help prise open the door for you. A good agent is well networked and should know when good jobs are coming up. He or she should know the employers well and get his or her clients ahead in the queue. An agent can blow your trumpet for you – it always sounds much better than when you blow your own trumpet yourself! An agent can be more aggressive with a potential employer than you can (unless you want to be taken on by someone who will grudgingly remember that you think an awful lot of yourself!).

A good agent can usually get you the best deal for a job. It's much easier to think and negotiate dispassionately about a deal if you're not so tied up with eagerness to get the job. The ability to get more money and better conditions, of course, is why a lot of employers hate agents and try to refuse dealing with them. (If only they realized how the agent can be used to positive effect by an employer – say, to improve work productivity, straighten out occasional problems, work with them to improve performances, or keep someone happy when the work boat is rocking!)

An agent can help develop and manage your career, but getting an agent can be very tricky unless you have already developed a career!

Sometimes it's easier to get your first few days' work as a presenter than it is to get an agent!

Agents are probably the most maligned people in the light entertainment industry. But the most important fact to remember is that *you* employ *them*, they do not employ you.

In practice the job of agent is not straightforward. The functions of agent, booker and manager get mixed up. Agents are sometimes all three, to which might be added the job of impresario on occasion, and also contractor when an agent is dealing with a specific event, particularly in the corporate field.

How Good Are You?

Hiring an agent is not a magical way of taking average or mediocre talent and selling it up to a better job. There are no miracles in television or radio. Having an agent, even a 'designer' agent, doesn't fool a hiring producer. It doesn't work that way. Cream still rises to the top!

THE PROFESSIONAL'S VIEW – JON ROSEMAN

Jon Roseman is acknowledged as one of the top agents in television presenting. He worked first as a Producer on the LWT programme *Weekend World* and forgets why he became an agent. 'It wasn't for the money,' he insists.

'No one really knows what makes a good presenter,' he says. 'If you put ten producers in a room and showed them five different presenters they would each have a different idea about who fits the bill.' Roseman is in the lucky position of being able to pick and choose his clients and rarely takes on someone who doesn't have some sort of track record. When a potential client contacts his organization, usually in writing with a CV and showreel, he aims to reply to them within a week. If you've included a showreel you can expect a few helpful hints in the reply.

'Not everyone needs an agent,' he says. 'If you're in regular work that precludes you doing anything such as advertising, voice-overs or corporate videos then you probably won't benefit from having an agent.'

People who benefit from having representation include those who can work outside their regular contract and those who are constantly looking out for work because they have short-term contracts.

'I see the agent–client relationship like a marriage,' he says. 'I have to like them if I'm going to work with them.'

Choosing the Right Agent

Obtaining an agent is an individual choice and often circumstances dictate the appropriate time. The decision to hire an agent needs to be viewed as one of the most critical decisions of your career.

The relationship between artist and agent *is* a bit like a marriage. It must be founded on trust, and there is a constant danger of resentment on both sides. But I have to return to the fact – artists employ the agent to find them work. There is an agreement, usually lasting a fixed period of time, on the expiry of which the artist can find another agent. An agent is under no obligation to take a presenter on to his or her books: he or she may already have a number of performers of the same type already.

For all that, the agent is often the engine room of the business. It is his or her job to find openings for clients on their list and to be always increasing their group of contacts. It is therefore in their interests to be out and about continually, going to showcases and parties, visiting venues and meeting potential employers.

Many agents find themselves specializing in specific areas of the business, for instance television, radio or theatre, cruising, clubs, holiday centres and the corporate field. Others book particular types of artist, and there are those who deal with television and radio almost exclusively.

One important quality in an agent is the amount of power he or she has. A powerful agent has influence, lots of good industry relationships, and other clients who are in demand. Ideally, you will be represented by an agent whose agency logo and own name carry a certain cachet. This does take time of course, most top agents won't really look at you until you are a name in your own right, but if you hang in and you have the talent, then you will work your way up there.

The thing to do is shop around. Don't just talk to one agent: get a feel for what each of them can do, how well they know your branch of the business, who else they have on their books, what they think of your 'act' and how they feel you might improve it.

The best way to approach an agent is the most simple and direct one. Start with either a phone call or a friendly and informative letter enclosing a CV and showreel. Awards, distinctions, articles by or about you or other biographical information is helpful, but don't go over the top: no bumper packages, it's too much for the agent and makes you look a little insecure – your talent and personality will sell you, you just need to give the agent a taster. One fellow agent told me that he feels an introduction via a mutual friend or a respected broadcast executive is also very helpful and beneficial to the initial process.

When you go to see them, treat it exactly as if you were going for a job. Put your interview gear on and be prepared to explain everything about yourself, personal details as well. You may want to have secrets from the press and your lover, but don't try to hide things from your agent. Your relationship has to be built on absolute openness and you should expect honesty in return – your agent will need to be frank about your voice, your looks, your clothes, your hair, your weight. Don't expect to like them all the time!

MIKE'S WISE WORDS – 17

Always be courteous to the agents that you see. Even if you don't get taken on, they may remember you when a particular job crops up and get in touch. If you have seen five agents and agreed terms with one, make sure the others know. And try to leave them on good terms – you never know when you might want to change your mind! Also, it will help to get all your CVs and taped material back.

Meshing of Minds

The last main criterion for choosing an agent is that your agent sees you the same way that you see yourself. If you think you're a wholesome 'girl-next-door' type and you want to do work on educational programmes, but your agent keeps sending you to the Playboy Channel, then the relationship probably won't work.

I try to give everyone who writes to me some sort of response, if I can. I look at the tapes, listen to the CDs, read the CV, study the photograph. If I think I can help, or would like to know more, I arrange a meeting. This first meeting is as much about how we get on as about how good the person is. We chat about hopes and fears, plans for the future and so on. I want to assess whether I can do anything for them. It usually lasts just over half an hour. If it lasts five minutes – on either side – then the message is clear.

I never make a decision at the first meeting, but I try to follow up within a couple of days, letting the person know whether I'm interested or not and judging whether they are, too. If we agree that we might do business then we have another meeting and, after that, the terms between us are settled.

When you contact an agency, you must show promise and professionalism. An agent usually won't touch you if you haven't had any experience at all, so you will probably have to make a start on your own. However, if you are an ambitious newcomer, an appointment with an agent may well give you some invaluable pointers even if you don't get invited onto his or her books.

So What Do We Know Now?

- *Only 5 per cent of presenters' jobs get advertised – you need to do your homework and build your contacts*
- *It is harder than it looks – practice makes perfect*
- *Study the programmes you want to present carefully*
- *Agents don't get you work – you do*
- *You don't need an agent all the time, but the right one is a powerful ally*

CHAPTER 6

Television Presenting

Presenting Yourself

There are four ways of becoming a television presenter, according to private research done by the BBC. The first is by being an expert in a particular field, the second is through journalism, the third through being a 'wannabe' and the fourth through existing celebrity status. Clearly, most people will fall into the wannabe category. But the broadcasters have decided you need to be in at least two out of the four categories to stand a decent chance of success. So, are you an expert? Can you talk with knowledge, authority and feeling about history, gardening, cookery or DIY – just four of the specialist subjects which are turning ordinary people into television stars, such as Charlie Dimmock on gardening? Everyone has something they are interested in, as a hobby or a previous job, and there are ways to develop that interest into a recipe for stardom. Journalism is a real specialism and I deal with it specifically in another chapter, along with sport. Celebrity status – well, only you know if you already have that – could your name be Tara, or Elton, perhaps?

The Range of the TV Presenting Job

From sports reporters to game show hosts to war correspondents, the jobs vary wildly but there are certain characteristics and abilities presenters have in common. Energy, confidence and a positive mental attitude (after 15 takes of the same item!), you have to be fit, focused (it's one of the hardest jobs in the media to get into), happy to befriend anyone and have a real passion for the subject you are presenting. It's not easy work! If you want to follow this difficult and popular leg of broadcasting then be prepared for a struggle.

Important characteristics of presenters are charisma, attractiveness, enthusiasm, the ability to command respect, versatility and stretch-ability. Presenters need to be able to move around, multi-task and have multiple skills. Popular presenters are those who are not afraid to get their hands dirty, they are approachable, real people who interface with and understand their audiences.

Other Ways In

Rather than attempting to start as a presenter, I would suggest that you might want to just try getting into TV in any way. Many pre-senters start as a runner with a production company, expected to do everything and anything. If you're really lucky you'll be paid, but you may have to turn up for nothing until you can prove yourself invaluable. See it as a learning curve: you can see how programmes are put together and what the presenter's responsibilities are on and off-screen. Make sure you are punctual, enthusiastic and flexible – you want to be on hand when the presenter is off sick so that you can fill in! But watch out for the exploiters out there – if you're still only making the tea after six months then maybe it's time to move on.

Think about starting as a secretary, marketing officer, assistant or similar for a big TV channel or production company. You may then be able to move sideways within the company into that presenting post that you always wanted. You'll also build up contacts within the industry, as well as valuable knowledge and skills. But you could be a secretary for a long time, so don't lose sight of where you want to be.

MIKE'S WISE WORDS – 18

Lateral thinking – it pays to get your foot through the door, in whatever capacity you can. Katy Hill, who became a celebrated presenter on the Saturday morning BBC show *Live and Kicking*, began work there as secretary to the Head of BBC Children's Programmes. Whilst in her keyboard job, she submitted her showreel to the editor of *Blue Peter*. While she was waiting to hear she wrote to the bosses at the Nickelodeon channel, who gave her the break she was after. With the direct TV experience with Nickelodeon under her belt, Katy got an audition for *Blue Peter*, and the rest, as they say, is history!

Commercials

Working on commercials is another way into the mainstream TV business. Commercials are almost entirely commissioned by advertising agencies, many of which now have full-time production departments. However, for casting they generally use agents, some of whom specialize in this field, so it is as well that you find out who they are through directories and the advertising trade press. You will find some useful contact details in Chapter 14.

Unless the advertiser demands a star name, producers of commercials are inclined to employ lesser-known faces, so the chances are good for unknowns to break into this field, especially if they are quick learners. Some commercials are very elaborate and expensive, using dancers, singers and a choreographer, but the majority are shot in a day or two. There is also a great opening for voices on radio ads. If you can land a role in a TV or radio advert then it gets your voice heard and/or face seen on screen; then you can start worming your way into the subconscious of the watching and listening public.

Corporate Videos
Another way in through the side door! Many companies use corporate videos, either to communicate a message to their customers, such as a demonstration of how a product works, or to communicate new working methods and practices to their employees. In industries where rules can change fairly frequently, such as in banking or building societies, or where products change, like a new model of a motor car, companies find it easier to give their employees a video to watch.

Say that Bombay Cash Registers have had to produce a kit to adapt their machines to cope with a new currency (like the euro). A presenter would be hired to demonstrate, in front of a video crew, how the old cash registers can be adapted. The whole thing would be scripted like a television programme, and filmed in exactly the same way. Copies of the tape would then get sent out to Bombay's engineers, who would be able to view how the adaptation is done by watching the demonstration and listening to the presenter's explanation.

The same presenter and video crew might also be asked to make a special video for customers of Bombay who would need to know how the cash register is used after the adaptation has taken place. And Bombay Cash Registers would probably send out the video to customers in a nice, specially designed package with a brochure for new machines as well.

Many companies use this method to keep employees and customers informed, and the money for presenters is often quite healthy. Some companies, especially transnationals, also do live magazine programmes for their staff who might view the programmes on special closed-circuit screens before starting work for the day. Such a programme might feature an interview by the presenter with the Chairman of the company who would answer employees' questions from all around the world. This is terrific training for new presenters, without exposing them to really mass audiences. Any mistakes are made in front of relatively small numbers of people. (But, of course, we don't make mistakes, do we?)

Corporate Entertainment
Another area in which to build your expertise. Corporate entertainment was summed up by one specialist in this field as 'entertainment that people haven't paid to see'. To which he might have added, 'and often don't want to'.

Those invited to a corporate event, whether it be a dinner, product launch, celebratory gathering or a family fun day organized by a company or organization are, frankly, there to receive a message from the host company. Product launches, for example, usually require the presence of a presenter, often from television and not always an entertainer, to introduce and possibly compere the proceedings. The events occasionally incorporate a spectacular theatrical element, employing dancers and a choreographer who devises a theme based around the product.

Dinners, on the other hand, need a first-class and occasionally well-known speaker, though this is not always the case. Many people from outside the entertainment profession have developed considerable skill at after-dinner speaking, and earn large fees. Again, this helps to build up your presentation and audience-handling skills, as well as giving you material for your showreel.

MIKE'S WISE WORDS – 19

The more skills you can offer the more likely it is that you will stay in employment. The power of the various broadcasting unions has decreased considerably over the last 10 years in the UK. Years ago a television sound recordist could have caused a walk-out if he so much as moved an electrician's light on location. These days, most television stations have trained sound people to rig lights as part of their jobs, and have allowed electricians to train as sound recordists. The opportunity is there now to learn several disciplines at once, which makes you much more valuable as an employee.

Other Proxy Jobs

Looking further afield, you can get work in a theatre, cinema or in, say, children's entertainment, which could help prepare you for the little screen.

Children's entertainers have to be able to do a little bit of everything – verbal comedy, clowning, magic, puppetry, balloon modelling, cartooning, juggling, paper-tearing, face-painting and ventriloquism, as well as being capable of organizing games and competitions. Much of the work of the children's entertainer is in private houses and hired function rooms, and is obtained mainly by word-of-mouth and personal contact.

It is possible to vary this in a number of ways. Even the smallest holiday centre is likely to employ a children's entertainer two or three times a week, and the bigger ones use them as an important part of the entertainment team. They can also be found on cruise ships.

Don't forget either that there are many hours of children's entertainment on television each week. Producers are always on the lookout for new ideas.

Promote Yourself

Finally, be prepared to network. Join groups and clubs, check out Internet discussion groups and mailing lists like *Shooting People* and *Exposure* ... or start one yourself. The more skills and contacts you can develop, the better.

Do web searches, check out who is advertising for production staff and offer yourself as a runner. Note down companies that make programmes that you watch, with presenters you like, and send them your CV. Review all your skills and knowledge and target those production companies that specialize in making programmes that you have particular knowledge in – you will have more to offer them.

THE PROFESSIONAL'S VIEW – DONAL MACINTYRE

Donal Macintyre, star of BBC 1's *Wild Weather* and *Macintyre Undercover*, went into reporting through journalism in his native Ireland. He began reporting for the BBC in 1994 and was given a job on ITV's *World in Action* shortly after. Earning his stripes on that programme led to him being recruited by BBC 1's Controller, Peter Salmon, to create *Macintyre Undercover*.

Donal stresses the importance of cross-genre skills in presenters.

A presenter who can switch between different sorts of

programmes will do far better than a one-trick pony. A good presenter has credibility in more than one area.

And never forget, treat people how you would like to be treated, respect people and look out for who you meet on the way up – you may meet them on the way back down and they may be in a position to help you. Be enthusiastic and likeable and treat people with dignity and you'll get the best opportunity to make the most of chances that come your way.

The Tools of The Trade

If you're going to try to get yourself noticed as a presenter you're going to have to equip yourself with certain things. Three essentials are a CV, a showreel and well-produced photographs. I address the question of CV writing in Chapter 13. But integral to wanting to be a TV presenter is the need to show people what you look like – in still and motion pictures.

Television Showreels

One of the most important tools for a presenter, possibly the most important, is a showreel. I have said elsewhere that, even after several hundred years in the business, I still find it difficult to 'imagine' what someone will look like on camera. Therefore, it's no good storming into a producer's office and demanding to be put on the screen – you have to prove to them what you will look like and what makes you stand out from all the other wannabes. The very best of ways is to demonstrate it with a showreel.

A showreel is, typically, a four or five minute long video showing you at your presenting best. When you've been in the business for a short while you can have your showreel made from clips of things that you have done. Until then you are going to have to find alternative ways of showing yourself on camera.

I often say that it is not easy to replicate the dynamic of a live television show, and have occasionally advised against making show-reels specially. But, if you haven't done anything on television yet, and you want to show yourself in action, then having one made specially is an option.

There's a wide variety of ways of making a showreel yourself. You could use a home video camera and get a friend just to film you speaking to camera for a couple of minutes. Or you could try assembling some essential bits to make it look as though you have done certain things – a mock interview, a piece-to-camera, a newscast, a studio presentation, etc. You can get these professionally made, but they do cost.

A showreel is often a by-product of those one-day TV Presenter Training Courses that you see advertised in the Media *Guardian* or *Broadcast* magazine. Normally they include interviewing techniques, voice training, reading autocue and wardrobe advice. Make sure you choose one that gives you a showreel at the end. These courses do cost; you can shell out anywhere between £60 and £700 with no guarantee that you'll succeed. For a day of training plus a showreel you'll be looking at spending at least £500. It seems like a lot of money, but you won't be taken seriously in the business without a showreel to your name.

MIKE'S WISE WORDS – 20

I have always reckoned that a producer or casting director makes up their mind about someone on a showreel within the first few seconds of viewing. That means you have to shock or amuse someone within a very short time. If they like you or are intrigued, they'll view a bit more, and then if they like that they might ask for more material or request that you come and see them. The old theatrical adage 'Leave them wanting more' is worth bearing in mind. I've seen people use an out-take (a failed shot) or a rude bit at the start of their showreel, or even a shot of them as a baby. One girl even put her mum on the front saying what a good presenter the daughter was! (It would have served her right if her mum got the job instead!)

When making your showreel, bear in mind the person who is going to watch it. Yours could be one of several hundred that the recipient has to watch. So you need to grab attention with virtually the first frame and then hold the attention without the viewer drifting off to sleep. Make your showreel the best you possibly can so it really shows what a cool and professional presenter you are when reading from autocue, interviewing and linking items, etc. Then mail it to those programmes and production companies that involve the presenting you want to do, along with a covering letter that illustrates your passion for presenting.

Make multiple copies of your showreel. A few stations may want to keep yours on file for future consideration. Make it easy for others to return the tape, but don't expect all of them to do so. Many tapes, unsolicited ones in particular, wind up in wastebaskets or recycling bins.

Most people put their showreel onto VHS – the format which nearly all domestic videos use. TV executives have such machines in their offices for what is known as **offline** viewing – that is, away from transmission standard machinery. However, we are moving into the digital era more and more, and it may be that you should consider a CD format, or even DVD, which people can view on their office or home computers. This digital format is also useful because it can readily be shipped by email or immediately used on one of the increasing number of 'showcase' web sites that are springing up.

Package the video nicely. Put a photo of yourself on the cover and add some biographical details so that, even if the accompanying letter ends up in the bin, your vital statistics and your address and phone numbers stay linked to your video. I have known some showreels stay on executive shelves for weeks and months and then suddenly produce a result when the executive needs a face or a voice in a hurry.

Photographs

A good still photo of you could be worth more than a lot of moving pictures. You should always send one with any job application. As I pointed out, some people put one on the front of the video case containing their showreel. It all serves to tempt a busy producer to watch and, while they might forget your name, the face will always serve to jolt their memory of what you look like and who you are.

The first step to getting great photos is to know your type. People need to know what they're getting when they call you in to audition. So, if you are not a model-type, please do not get glamorous headshots. But if you are gorgeous, let the viewer know. To get an idea of your type, watch TV and films for roles that you think you could have played. Ask your friends, family and fellow professionals how they see you being cast. (The most effective way to get straight answers on this, and the scariest, is to ask complete strangers.) Ask yourself things like are you upmarket or down in terms of how classy you look? Do you have a regional or ethnic flavour to your style? How cool or smart are you? How innocent or worldly are you? Are you a good guy or a bad guy? A great photo will answer all of these questions!

This means you need the right headshot. Compare prices and packages (some photographers will let you keep the negatives, some won't). Look at their book of sample photos before hiring them. Yes, it is their best stuff, but it can be revealing if it is not what you want. Look at lighting in their shots – make sure the eyes are lit, preferably with a single point of light. And look for personality and relaxation in the sample photos. It's worth getting it right.

For each role, a producer or casting director will receive hundreds or thousands of CVs and headshots, from which they will narrow the field to the number that they have the time and/or need to audition. There are so many presenters vying for so few roles in this field, where the supply so greatly exceeds the demand, that getting an audition is quite an achievement in itself and the photo could just be the clincher.

Get at least two different sorts of shots and make sure one is a full-length one. You will need to make a judgement as to which shot goes with which job application. Conventional wisdom holds that the more commercial shot should be smiley, and the traditional shot more serious, but this is an oversimplification. For both types of shot, think about how you will be cast and tailor the photo to that image. It is actually a good idea to have more than those two shots, just for variety. In the meantime, get one great photo reproduced for your main search (a minimum of 50 copies). Again this is an area where a digital copy of your photo is extremely useful – good for emailing, putting on web sites and for scanning onto the front cover of your video. Some processors will give you a full set of photos and a copy on CD as well, which increases the chance of maintaining the quality.

Auditions for TV Presenters

If your CV, photo and showreel have made it to the top of the pile and you're on the shortlist, the chances are they'll call you to come and audition. Even if they say they're just inviting you for interview, be prepared for a sudden and unexpected audition. Casting for pre-senters for a TV programme is often an in-depth affair with inter-views and screen tests to find the personality and star quality that the show requires.

MIKE'S WISE WORDS – 21

The reason companies will audition you, even if you have a great showreel, is that they want all their short-listed candidates to do exactly the same stuff on tape so that they can be properly compared with each other. Also, your showreel shows you at your best, but in live action you might need several takes to get it right, and an audition will show that up. Remember that audi-tions are, or should be, about your potential. It is what you have to offer that the audition is all about – not what you've already done and polished up.

Before the Audition

I always say to people who are up for a presenter's job – first, learn to pass the test. It's a bit like being a learner driver, what you are actually learning to do is pass the driving test. The hard bit, actually learning to drive, sitting on your own in the car, comes later. So it is with presenting.

You need to learn how to sell yourself to the buyers, the producers, directors and casting agents. There are techniques for getting through auditions that you might never use again in the real job, but there are little tricks you can learn which will impress the judges!

Be Prepared

It is a good idea to learn in advance as much as you can about the production for which are being auditioned. Sometimes the secretary who calls you for audition will give you minimal information, sometimes deliberately. Don't be afraid to call back and check out what you'll be expected to do. (Don't forget, the secretary may hanker after the job herself and be trying to put you off!)

So before you do anything else, find out the following:

- What is the programme about? DIY, history or a quiz?
- Who is the programme aimed at? Kids, the elderly, under 25s?
- What sort of person are they looking for? Educated middle class or rowdy clubbing youth?
- What is the 'whole picture' (and not just your part in it)?
- If the job is for one of the many new 'generic' channels, make sure you watch the channel and understand the scheduling patterns and presentation requirements.
- What exactly is expected of you personally?
- Who is doing the audition – what are their likes and dislikes? Can you work out a way of playing to these? (Even a simple thing like finding out about their favourite football team and commenting on it when you arrive can work.)
- When and where is the actual job taking place? (This seems obvious but some people turn up for the audition even though they won't be free at the time or cannot get to the place of actual filming).

Having found out the answers to each of these points, and any others you can think of, you can then sit back with the facts and work out what you should wear, what sort of makeup, whether you should have a posh voice or a friendly tone, etc.

The aim of an audition is to find out whether you as an individual are suited to the project. It's like a job interview; you look perfect on your CV, on paper, but maybe you are actually a really bad team player and you hate being questioned. So it is with an audition, your photo is perfect, your showreel is incredible, but you have a stammer on camera that prevents you from getting your message across clearly and concisely.

MIKE'S WISE WORDS – 22

I was once interviewed for a job where I felt the interviewer was going to be just 'going through the motions' as a favour to the Chairman of the company, whom I knew. I found out what I could about the interviewer. He was American and liked a particular type of broadcasting technique. I found out where his home town was, researched his favourite broadcaster and got tapes of the broadcaster concerned. When I went into the interview, after about 15 minutes, I just casually mentioned that I happened to know the man's home town and asked if he'd ever seen this particular broadcaster. Suddenly the room lit up – I was on this man's wavelength and we swapped stories about why his favourite broadcaster was the best in the world. That was it, I got the job.

Auditions for any project can be nerve-wracking. Many people go to them full of high hopes and sometimes come away embarrassed and feeling humiliated. Just remember this is a natural feeling – you've gone along to the event with a complete picture of who you are and someone you might never have met has pulled you and pushed you in all directions. Suddenly you feel like you're not in control of yourself and then that you haven't given a good account. Even the successful candidates come out of auditions feeling like wet rags – it is a demanding experience, your whole personality is on trial. Just remember, everyone else feels the same. If you gave your all to the event then just remain confident that **talent** will conquer all!

In most auditions you will be judged on what type you are. This is particularly the case for commercials, corporate videos and TV presenting. You can of course modify your appearance to fit different roles and different television companies. Whatever the job, you need to fit in to be at home in your surroundings.

On the day of your audition dress for success. If you want to present television pop music shows, then a trendy image will be essential, so that you look like you are one of the audience. A serious look is essential for news reading. It can help you to build a rapport. Make sure you feel comfortable and look the part. It also helps if you ask, in advance, what clothes they would like you to wear and what colours (don't forget you could clash with the scenery), and take a spare outfit if you can. It gives them a choice, but, more importantly, it shows that you respect their right to produce and direct you.

Never wear new clothes to an audition: you will feel uncomfortable and there may be itches in new fabrics. Anything like that will make you come across as uncomfortable and ill-at-ease. Don't eat a large meal or drink alcohol before the audition – it will make you feel full and woolly-headed.

Get there a good 15 minutes early so you have time to grab a cup of coffee, cool down from a hectic journey or dry off from a rainstorm. You can also use the time to chat to others up for the part, see what information they can give you and any gossip you may have missed out on.

In your audition you may be asked to use props. Even a microphone can feel uncomfortable if you are not used to using one so make sure you practise. Try using everyday items when you practise presenting: it could be a photo, brochure or toy. Presenters often use props so if you can feel at home talking to camera with any prop, then you're off to a head start.

Presenters typically wear an **earpiece** so that the producer can communicate directly with them. They will speak to you while you are talking, which can be off-putting. You need to practise wearing an earpiece so you get used to the feel of it. Think of it as eavesdropping on someone else's conversation. You could try wearing headphones with the radio on and practise listening and talking at the same time. It's not quite the same as a flustered producer screaming in your ear 'Say something! Anything!' but you will develop a feel for it.

Practise autocue reading. If you can't get to the real thing, remember you can fake it by writing a script on a computer, making the print large and double spacing it. Then just get someone to roll it up and down as they would in the studio. (The cursor – not the monitor!)

If you can get a look at the studio where the audition will take place then do. If not, take a look at the way the studio is laid out on similar programmes. What you want to get a feel for is what is called the **geography** of the studio.

In the Audition

The audition could be held in a variety of places. An actual studio would be nice, but sometimes a programme will save its budget by using an ordinary room or one of the special **rehearsal rooms** that are dotted around the main production centres. If it's an ordinary room, you might find the director has a camera set up on a tripod and is working it himself from a fixed position against a plain piece of scenery.

On the day there may be a casting director, camera operator and, possibly, a rep from your agency in the room. You will be told what to do and where to stand. Ask any questions that occur to you – don't guess, you could miss out on some important direction. Ask about your clothing and appearance; ask about the pace of speech delivery, etc.

Stand or sit where you will do your piece for a second and look around you. Can you see everything you need to? Is there a TV monitor which shows you what you look like? Is it in what's called your **eyeline**? If not, get it moved there. You have a peripheral field of vision. You may be looking straight at the camera but you can see a whole load of other things around it and your subconscious is taking it all in. Use that field of vision to your advantage. If you brought someone with you, you might be able to put him or her in your eyeline so that they can encourage you!

Is an autocue being used? Is it readable? If a camera with autocue tries to move in close on you, beware. With the camera too close you can be seen **scanning** the words, backwards and forwards (which looks shifty); it needs to be at least 10 feet away, so if the director wants a close-up he should leave the camera where it is and use a zoom lens. If the camera is too close, you'd be better off not using the autocue. Ask them to move the camera or turn off the autocue.

In the room or on the set you may also be introduced to people. Make eye contact with everyone to whom you are introduced; the idea is to look friendly and professional. Ensure you have a good handshake – firm but not too hard.

If you are videoed during the interview and are asked whether you would like to see the playback, say yes. It is embarrassing but you will learn a lot by seeing yourself on tape in a pressurized situation. At the end you may be asked if you have any questions; if so, only ask sensible intelligent questions. Have they got a schedule slot? What will be the competition on the other channels? Don't ask a question that could sound as if you don't know why you've been asked to audition – you should have done that before you agreed to come.

If you mess up, don't panic. Remember that, as a general rule, you'll be allowed a retake if you ask for it. If you get flustered just stop, say 'sorry, can I do that again?', and take your time. People are generally quite sympathetic, just be honest with them. Nerves are perfectly natural, even expected, especially if you are a newcomer to the camera lens. Always, unless otherwise directed, look into and speak to the camera lens so that when they run the tape after your audition, you'll seem to be talking directly to them.

Last, but by no means least: be yourself! Don't suddenly try to develop a different personality just for the camera. This is likely to just make you look a fake and unprofessional. The producer – and your viewers – will quickly see through it. Everyone has his or her own style, so just let it happen – in fact capitalize on it! Smile, enjoy it, have confidence in yourself, and let your personality shine through.

MIKE'S WISE WORDS – 23

When I was still at school in the North of England, I fancied myself as a TV presenter and heard about auditions for a TV rock and roll show that was re-casting its main anchors. I wrote off and found myself on the shortlist, invited down to London for a try-out. Well, I hitched a lift from my home 200 miles up the A6, and slept on a friend's floor in Earls Court before getting myself up in my best clothes and heading for the studios for my big chance. The 'short' list was, of course, agonizingly long, and we queued to file in front of the producer. We had to choose one of two people to interview, male or female – I chose the guy and, within seconds of sitting down to start the interview, and hardly clearing my throat, I heard a voice say: 'I think we've seen enough, thank you.' I can't even remember how I got out of there, I was so embarrassed. I walked around in a daze for at least an hour, trying to work out what I'd done 'wrong'. I felt seriously as though I'd been attacked and robbed of everything I held dear.

But I survived, and am here to tell you the tale of how, 30 years later; I was approached by the man who turned me down. He wanted me to represent him as an agent. Can I tell you how tempting it was to say, 'No thank you, I think I've heard enough . . .'? As they say in this business, 'What goes around, comes around . . .'

Chin Up

I've warned you about the sense of anti-climax that you might get when you emerge from a draining audition. Don't start casting around for people to blame – it all comes down to you in the end, and there are very few people that you can rely on 100 per cent to think about you and your problems all the time. You have to do it for yourself and learn what you need to ask in advance.

Never get down-hearted if you aren't chosen for a **recall**. You may have done a brilliant audition but there might be a million good reasons why they didn't want you. Don't take rejections to heart, and get right on with pushing for your next project. If you can, obtain a copy of your audition tape and run through it with someone you trust, your agent for instance, or loved one. Learn from each occasion and use it to build your confidence.

Never Give Up

If you want to be a television presenter, then do it. Never, ever, lose faith in yourself and always be prepared. You could be walking down the road, or just sitting in reception, and someone could spot you. You could be making a cup of tea, as a runner on a production, and someone could fail to turn up. Your big chance could come when you least expect it. Burn with ambition and never let anyone tell you it isn't going to happen. It will.

So What Do We Know Now?

- *You need to be more than a wannabe – you must also be either a journalist, or an expert, or a celebrity*
- *You need charisma, enthusiasm, attractiveness and versatility*
- *Be prepared to work anywhere in order to gain 'air miles'*
- *Make a good, surprising, short showreel to get yourself noticed*
- *Be prepared for auditions – do lots of homework on the people who are seeing you and the programmes they've made*
- *Be prepared for rejection – use it to build your determination*

CHAPTER 7

Radio Presenting

Who the Hell is That?

As I am sitting writing this chapter, someone has left the radio on in the background, and I realize that I have been listening sub-consciously to it for at least an hour. However, apart from the occasional favourite bit of music, I couldn't tell you a single thing that I've heard. Is that good or bad? What it does tell me is that the presenter has not impressed himself on my memory at all. I can tell you that he's male, but I don't know his name and I can't remember one thing that he's said that sticks in my mind.

Sadly, that's the way that a large amount of commercial radio is heard these days – and the bosses of the large radio groups seem to like it that way! As little speech as possible and as much music, as though they are afraid that speech might drive the listener away!

Of course, I am talking about a mainly music radio environment and there are some notable exceptions – Chris Tarrant on Capital Radio in London, Chris Evans when he has a radio programme, Daryl Denham on Virgin Radio, Chris Moyles on BBC Radio 1, and, for me the king of them all, now sadly no longer with us – Kenny Everett. Everett was a one-off and ran his Wireless Workshop Company almost as a hobby, producing some amazing radio work including the unforgettable Kaptain Kremen series. Listening to him was like being in a permanent drama improvization class.

What's The Job For You?

So what sort of a radio presenter do you want to be? Most young people immediately jump for the job of DJ – it sounds fun and it allows you to play music all day. But with technology taking all the studio operations workload, the job can be quite 'samey' once the novelty has worn off.

Most music radio presenters are limited to a specific number of minutes of speech each hour, and they're in trouble with the **PD** (programme director) if they exceed the limit. Of course, it does concentrate the mind and make you really work hard at what you say if you only have four minutes an hour to talk.

Presenters do get more chance to talk on other stations, of course. There are the speech radio stations: SportsTalk Radio (which started out at as Talk Radio) is the national commercial speech station, and there's London News Radio with its two news channels. Then there are the BBC's stations – Radios 4, 5 and 7 and the various local radio stations dotted around the country. So the opportunity to talk and get your personality across on radio does exist.

Radio news, current affairs and documentary work can be extremely rewarding since, unlike television, you can actually be your own presenter, producer and editor rolled into one. The technology is such that you can carry a small recorder with you, do interviews, record **voiceovers** and edit fairly large amounts of programme material almost anywhere. And the glory of that – again unlike television – is that if you can stump up the cash for a decent recorder, you're already in business.

There are a number of people who make a decent living out of making series of programmes for radio from their home studios. And I know of at least one nationally known DJ who has his own home-based studio where he can do complete radio shows, live, with music, to a number of different stations all over the country, thanks to the wonders of ISDN.

MIKE'S WISE WORDS – 24

You've probably encountered quite a lot of radio presenters and reporters in quite intimate circumstances – although it's likely that you didn't know it at the time!

Many national radio reporters have ISDN lines and radio booths in their homes, which enable them to participate in news and current affairs programmes while still in their pyjamas. And some of the top freelance radio presenters also have equipment which enables them to record voiceovers and short radio commercials **down the line** to any radio studio in the world, again thanks to ISDN. One well-known national presenter has a special booth in his house where he conducts a phone-in for an hour a week on a national radio station, without stirring from his home comforts!

Avoid Meaningless Banter

The reason the term 'DJ' has so many negatives attached to it is because many times DJs say meaningless things. Too much of what is said on the radio does not deliver a listener benefit. It is important to sound knowledgeable about the artists and songs.

Here are some key needs of the listener:

- Song titles and artists.
- Special promotions, contests, shows and features the station is running.
- Personality that is genuine, interesting, entertaining and informative.
- Traffic problems in the area.
- The time.

Getting In

Again, nothing can beat the work experience route for getting you into the right environment and obtaining the best picture of what goes on in a radio studio. And, again, it puts you in the right place to be called on at short notice to stand in for people who might not be able to do the job – either because they haven't turned up, or because their voice has gone missing!

MIKE'S WISE WORDS – 25

A radio presenter's voice is their most important asset. So don't go begging for jobs or doing work experience with a cold or some other voice-threatening disease. I once got a placement in a radio station for a young client who, unknown to me, suffered from repeated viral laryngitis. She turned up on her first day croaking and coughing and wondered why the station boss immediately sent her home and made no arrangements for her to come back!

As in other branches of broadcasting, the first thing you've got to do is show interest in the business. Don't just listen to the radio, really pay attention to what's happening on the programmes that you'd like to work on. Think about how the presenters are styling themselves, what they're saying, how they use the time available to them to get their message over. What is attractive about them? Why is one presenter more 'listenable to' than another is? Are accents such as Irish or 'mid-Atlantic' more user-friendly than others? Could you adjust your voice to cope?

Listen to the voice **cadence** of a particularly successful presenter. To me, both Chris Tarrant and Chris Evans have voices that sound like excited schoolboys. The voice is always on the up-tilt and 'eager', they speak quickly and are also at the top of their 'register'. This is unlike, say, the actor Christopher Price, whose slow, base voice is used for voiceover work mainly when they want to scare the life out of you. Base tones are good for sober, serious news work. Higher register voices tend to be more user-friendly, fun and more suitable for entertainment and kids' programmes, etc. Some people, like the actor Martin Jarvis (who does a lot of radio work, especially story telling), have voices which can pitch up or down. There's real money in those sort of voice boxes.

Record yourself presenting in the way that you believe makes you sound good. Get other people to listen and to give you a genuine appraisal of how you sound to them. Ask your friends, especially: they'll tell you whether your radio voice is different from how they hear you normally, and which voice they like.

Try recording different forms of presentation to give yourself an idea of where your style of voice would fit best. You need to play to your strengths. If you sound good reading the news or interviewing someone and your voice isn't as comfortable introducing pop music, then you'll begin to understand how others will cast you.

THE PROFESSIONAL'S VIEW – DARYL DENHAM

Daryl Denham, one of music radio's rising – or risen – stars, with a breakfast show on the national commercial station Virgin Radio, has no doubt that the secret of his success is straight-forward – hard work and enthusiasm.

At 13, with 'hugely encouraging parents', Daryl was running his own mobile disco and regularly doing weekend gigs at parties. Music was a fun subject at school and he wrote songs for his school group, but he always imagined himself working on the support side of the music industry, maybe as a record plugger.

At 16, he was volunteering at his local hospital radio station – 'I gained really valuable experience there from people who knew what they were talking about' – and did spare-time work at a local record shop, all the while sending out demo tapes to station programme directors.

He landed a job as an in-store disc jockey at a chain store and then was invited to Invicta FM in Kent, where he arrived for interview on the Friday to find that someone had just resigned. By Monday he was at the microphone in a new job. 'I wouldn't say it was just luck,' he says, 'but also through constantly working at the business as much as I could. That meant that I was ready to start the moment I was given an opportunity.'

Daryl has also worked on the speech side, producing an award-winning series for BBC Radio 5 Live called *How Radio Won the War*. 'I was pleased to be able to show that I could do programmes that really had an effect on people, as well as doing music shows which, let's face it, fade away the moment you've finished them. I reckon with my morning show, if I can help people face the day with a smile, I've done my job.'

His worst moment was helping out as an overnight 'swing jock' on one station and falling asleep at the microphone. 'I woke up an hour later at 5 a.m. with all the phones flashing and decided that the best thing to do was just put on another piece of music and forget what I'd done. I thought I'd get the sack – but never heard any more about it.'

So, even in his silent moments Daryl Denham pleases his listeners!

Your Audio Showreel

When you decide it is time to audition for the radio presenter's job you will need to be armed with you CV and, most importantly, your radio showreel. Normally, a showreel is clips of some of the best stuff you've done and some typical presenting work. But if you haven't started yet then you won't have any archive tapes, unless you've worked on hospital, school or college radio. If you don't have any stuff at all then you're going to have to fake it.

You don't really need to worry about going into a studio. The showreel can be put together quite simply with a recorder and microphone (modern equipment usually gives a clear output), but if you can get access to a **DAT** machine then it will sound more professional. The finished tape can be transferred to CD, tape or mini disk; I would go for CD or tape though, because that way the radio station manager can listen to you wherever he or she is. Most cars have either a CD or tape player or both, mini disk players are less common and you want to make it really simple for your future employer.

Most PCs will allow you to record onto re-writable CDs, however, if this is not possible, a premium-quality cassette will suffice perfectly well. A demo tape that has obviously been done using a cheap microphone and an old tape recorder will not be received with the same enthusiasm as one recorded with decent equipment, care and attention. If you decide that you really want to use a professional studio then there are plenty around that you can hire for a couple of hours. You can find out where to go for information on studios in Chapter 14. Recording in a live studio demonstrates that you have had some **flying hours**, if nothing else.

Rules for Your Audio Showreel

There are a few important rules to follow when putting together your radio showreel.

1. Never allow it to run over five minutes; many people will only listen to the first minute. The major point of your demo is to leave the listener wanting more, so don't be afraid to send a demo with just three or four links.
2. Get to know the style of the station you are targeting so you introduce and play the right sort of music and are as casual or formal as they would expect from their own DJs.
3. Be careful about recording scripted pieces of 'spontaneous chat' onto your showreel; producers can tell if you are reading from a well-rehearsed script.
4. It's a good idea to mention the station between songs. If you are targeting one station then only mention that one, if not then it is quite acceptable to make up your own **station id** (identification) as it shows awareness of the marketing values of a radio station.
5. Ensure that you mention your own name every so often as it serves to remind the listener who you are, but make sure you have one way of saying your name, the station name and frequency, and stick to it.
6. ID the station clearly and regularly.
7. Make sure you link the tunes together on the tape. Play the first few seconds of the track, cut to the last few seconds and **back ref** (refer) about the song or band.
8. If you have the equipment handy then it sounds professional to finish a track at full volume before you go straight into the next, then fade the volume so you can speak over an instrumental lead in.
9. This is your one chance to prove to the listening employer that they need you on their radio station. Show how multi-talented you are – introduce competitions, make something

up, play a track and have a friend pretend to call in. Show how you can be authoritative yet friendly. You could also record the news off the radio and copy it onto tape so that you can introduce it; you could do the same with weather reports and traffic updates.

10. Sound like you really enjoy the music you're playing. A negative comment on the music is never useful, so every on-air opinion about a song must always be positive. A negative comment only makes you sound like you're on the wrong station. Negative comments can offend a listener but positive ones rarely do. Also you never know who might be listening and refuse to be interviewed on the station because of the comments you made ... Always smile: smiles can be heard!

MIKE'S WISE WORDS – 26

Getting listeners to keep their radios tuned to your entire show is the aim of every radio presenter. You need to learn to tempt your listeners. They need only to flick a switch or turn a dial if you start to bore them, and they may never return. Don't give your rival the gift of your audience! Despite the importance of leads and teases, many radio journalists do not understand how to fashion effective **hooks** to keep listeners tuned in. Listening to the radio is a private experience, so make your listeners feel involved. Imagine that you only have one listener (but stay away from the 'dear listener' cliché) and broadcast to that person and that person alone. Get a picture in your head of who your target listener is. Use this picture as a filter for all your ideas and output. Many seasoned broadcasters imagine that they're talking to a favourite aunt – or even their mum. It helps to develop a conversational style with your listener, and you might discover that many of them are answering you back in their own homes – although you'll never hear them!

Depending on what you are aiming for, your showreel may need an interview with someone (know anyone famous?), a straight read of the news bulletin and possibly a made-up advert or short story. I occasionally advise my clients to have more than one showreel for different sorts of job applications.

Your demo tape must be clearly labelled. Make sure you include on the cassette label or CD cover your name and address and a contact number, preferably a mobile number so they can be assured that you will be easy to get hold of. They won't want to chase you through work, your mum or your girl or boyfriend. Clearly indicate the duration of the showreel like this: if it is three minutes and twelve seconds long, 3' 12". Also ensure that the date corresponds with your cover letter – it makes it look as though you have made this tape very recently and just for the station to which you are applying.

Hopefully the audio showreel will get you noticed by the programme controller and get you into the station. But before you get on-air you may have to do some more demos to prove you can work to the standard the station requires. Therefore, as with your CV, your demo tape should make the programme controller desperate to meet you.

Enthusiasm is very important! Be bright, alive and 'into' the show. Talk about what's going on locally that a listener would like to get involved in, participate in, go to or see.

Speak in a 'right-to-the-point' manner. Don't tell your listener you're going to tell them something . . . just tell them! Be relatable and personable. Identify with the listeners' mood and try to empathize with what's happening in the listeners' world. Read the day – what's the weather like? Have there been any disasters that will affect the mood of your listeners?

MIKE'S WISE WORDS – 27

Record yourself. It is the most efficient way of improving how you sound, by critically listening back to what you said and how you said it, and then making an effort to improve it. Presenters who have been doing gigs for years still regularly request **RoT**s of their shows so they can hear what they sound like. Constructive critiquing of your broadcast output is always a good idea. While I do think it's up to the programme director to take the lead in this area, I also strongly advise every broadcaster to check out their own shows as often as possible. Are you communicating well? Are you name checking the station often enough? Is what you say making sense and is it worth listening to – or do you just sound as if you like the sound of your own voice?

Getting Into Radio

Some people have found their way into radio presenting in strange ways. I wouldn't recommend this, but there are a few people around in radio who got there by listening, avidly to the programme they wanted to work on, entered every competition (having to use fake names eventually as the presenters began to recognize them) and one day calling up, as themselves, and asking to have lunch with the presenter. Admittedly we may be venturing into stalking territory here, but as long as you don't scare anyone and get the message when they tell you to stop calling the station, being straightforward can get you good results.

But the best way to get into radio is to get that showreel sorted out. Package it up neatly with some details of yourself on the cover, write a nice letter and send it out to as many programme directors as you can. Ask for feedback, so that even if you don't get to see someone, you learn why they didn't think you were right. Don't be put off by anyone who says you'll never do it – the most important qualities are enthusiasm and persistence, and if you display those for long enough you'll get your foot in the door and onto the ladder of fame.

So What Do We Know Now?

- *Your speech time might be short – make the most of anything you say*
- *Avoid meaningless banter – think about what's important to the listener*
- *Use your voice to its full potential*
- *Put together a classy showreel tape or CD*
- *Listen back to yourself regularly*

CHAPTER 8

Broadcast Journalism and Sport

They'll Never Kill Off The Live Programme!

One area where your career is certain to have greater longevity is if you work in the areas that have to be broadcast live – live events, of course, and great state occasions are all likely to survive the great revolution that's going on in our midst. The audience will always want what we call a 'shared experience', such as watching football matches at the same time as their mates, or witnessing a major event like the funeral of Princess Diana. The knowledge that you're watching or listening to this event along with thousands, or millions, of your countrymen and women enhances your viewing experience. Another such area is the live broadcasting of news. On most of the major national broadcasters, news is broadcast live. Occasionally, some of the 24-hour news channels use recorded chunks of material as they go through the wee small hours of the night, but there's always a newscaster on duty in case of a breaking story. Work in the newsroom and you'll always be needed!

We Must Have News!

All broadcasters and their **regulatory bodies** see news and current affairs as an important part of their programming schedule. The BBC remains a major provider of this sort of programming with *Newsnight*, *Panorama* and its main news programmes. Channel 4 also provides an excellent news service on weekday evenings. In the mornings the news service is more light-hearted and softer, with shows like *GMTV* on ITV and Princess Production's *RI:SE* or Planet 24's *Big Breakfast*.

Broadcasters are doing all that they can to make news in a 'popular/ tabloid' way in an effort to attract young people.

Broadcast journalism is, of course, a huge field with many separate specialisms from local radio reporter through to anchor person for a network TV station's main nightly news programme. Whatever part of broadcasting you work in as a journalist, you will be responsible for researching, interpreting and communicating key news issues and events. For many, journalism is seen as a vocation, and it is their passion for recording and reporting on news and current affairs that carries them forward in a challenging and often tough career.

Qualities You Will Need

Broadly, you will have to study journalism and be an able and keen communicator. You will need to develop a **news sense**; coupled with the ability to explain often complex stories to a TV or radio audience that demands a quick fix of news. Self-starters and highly motivated individuals do well, but this needs to be tempered with a willingness to work as part of a team. Good journalists thrive on hard work and no sleep!

Career Path

How do you start and where can you go with it? This is an area where I strongly believe that university or college courses can be of positive help. The complexities of British law, the constitution, the need for varying skills such as languages, writing techniques, keyboard skills, layout knowledge, all need time for study. After that, it is fairly common to spend time on a work experience basis at either a local radio station or on newspapers. This is usually where you make your decision to begin to specialize in either print or broadcast fields. In television your first job could be as a sub-editor in a regional **newsroom**, or possibly researching on a current affairs or factual magazine show. Many newcomers have degrees in English, media studies or even history, and they then move on to newspapers or magazines to gain practical experience. For those without such experience and qualifications there are possibilities in news traineeships or trainee research. At the higher level, jobs include the editing of 'heavyweight' news programmes and then into senior management roles within broadcasting institutions.

The Journalistic Workplace

A large number of journalists are employed on news programmes – many will never be seen on screen but will work behind scenes compiling news stories, researching, writing and interviewing.

A typical television newsroom will have an Editor, an Editor-of-the-Day, a Producer-of-the-Day, a 'copy-taster' (to read and decide on the importance of incoming stories), a chief sub-editor and several sub-editors (sometimes called news assistants or news producers). There are also researchers, reporters, a Presenter-of-the-Day, a film/video organizer, several camera teams and video editors, a Director and a studio with relevant staff, such as vision mixers, production assistant, sound operators, etc. Sometimes there will be make-up facilities and wardrobe (although many studios and programmes have dispensed with this now). There will also be library facilities – video, sound effects and reference material – and a news-planning section to keep a forward planning diary and also to make sure obituaries of famous people are up to date! International newsrooms will also have a Home Editor, a Foreign Editor and **intake** facilities for handling reporters' incoming material.

The BBC and the commercial sector both have regional and national television and radio studios. At the regional studios local news bulletins are put together for that region and they will generally only be broadcast to their specific area. However, some stories in regional areas become relevant to the nation as a whole, and national newsrooms then use their regional counterparts to feed local stories which have wider implications for the rest of society. Such local stories can often be **worked up**. For example, a story about a local joyriding teenager can spawn national outrage, leading to spin-off interviews and calls for crackdowns on young offenders. The story may break in Southampton where BBC South is based, so the piece will be put together there. In this case the national newsreader would introduce the story and then hand over to BBC South with words like 'And here's more from our Southampton studios.' This, of course, is a key moment in the regional newsreader's career and life!

The Radio Newsroom

A radio newsroom will be much smaller, and some local stations have only two or three journalists on the staff. Working in a local newsroom is hard work, often quite a solo operation and can be repetitive. On the other hand, your material is often the most up-to-date and informative being slotted into a live programme, and a breaking story can be exhilarating to follow through on air as it unfolds.

Stories Abroad

If such a story breaks overseas, most major television stations will have correspondents stationed in key areas around the world: Hong

Kong, Paris, New York and so on. They will post correspondents if a particular story requires it – for example, an outbreak of war.

News Agencies

There are also **news agencies**, with Reuters, Press Association (PA) and Associated Press amongst the best known. They gather news from around the world through a network of news bureaux. Most news organizations subscribe to more than one such agency. These agencies work on a fairly simple basis of connections: a news agency bureau in Paris will have a strong link with sources in the President's office, the parliament, stock exchange and key government ministries such as the foreign office. The same happens with bureaux in every country across the world, resulting in a non-stop, finger-on-the-pulse news feed. The agency's journalists will put together these stories and send them down the **wires** to subscribers over the world.

There are television equivalents of these written word agencies – Reuters TV, APTV and WTN, for instance, have bureaux which employ camera teams and reporters around the world and supply pictures and reports on satellite feeds which occur several times a day. Some of the national state broadcasters also have **sharing agreements** which mean that, for instance, ABC in America will supply the BBC in the UK with material, and vice versa.

MIKE'S WISE WORDS – 28

The term 'wire' refers to the time when stories used to arrive down telegraph wires in the form of signals which would then be interpreted by huge typewriter-like machines – teleprinters – as words onto rolls of paper. Now, of course, written stories are sent on screen by Internet or similar and only printed out when needed. News agencies provide all sorts of services including general news and sports results, showbiz gossip, up-to-the-minute financial news and **rip 'n' read** bulletins. You can subscribe to a less detailed version of these **wire services** by clicking onto their web sites – Press Association even has a talking automated newsreader (Annanova) on its home page.

The Low Down on Journalism

As you can see, journalists can work in a variety of centres, and they can work on-screen or off. They can work on news or current affairs programmes and can also be very important in documentary programming. News journalists can work behind the scenes in the studios putting the news bulletins together, they can appear on-screen in the studio as newscasters, or they may go out on location as reporters and send in filmed reports.

Hours can be very unsociable; if there is a major air crash at three in the morning reporters have to get 'on the road' or into the studio to cover it, whilst other journalists on call have to put the stories together. Journalists always have a large contact book in which they list useful names and numbers: politicians, police, doctors, experts in particular fields and celebrities. If a really major story happens, news organizations have systems in place to alert all their staff and call them into the news centre instantly. The journalistic ethos is such that the problem is often keeping employees away from the studio during a major **breaking story** so that there are sufficient well-rested people to carry on with news production on the next shift!

Dedicated News Channels
Several news organizations around the world have solved the 24–hour nature of the job by creating dedicated news channels in TV and radio. This means that there is always a team of people scheduled on at any time of day or night – Sky News, BBC News 24 and the ITN News Channel are all examples. Some international broadcasters also plan to practise what is known as the **sunrise newsroom** system. This is where the production of news takes place in three locations around the world – say, London, Washington and Sydney – with each location taking an eight-hour shift during their daylight hours before passing production responsibility on to the next time zone.

Producing the News
Production of news programmes is usually in a studio based alongside the newsrooms. The production **gallery** or control room will be close by as well. However, with technological development, news and news programmes can now be broadcast from almost anywhere in the world. Sometimes, as with the events in the USA on 11 September 2001, or the death of Princess Diana, news teams will locate mobile studios close to the scene of the action and presenters will be seen closely involved with what is happening.

On **outside broadcasts**, as in the studio, a gallery is needed with the three components of engineering, production and sound. In another nearby truck will be recording facilities for videotape manned by **VT** operators and engineers. If it is a live transmission, a further vehicle manned by engineering staff is involved. Their task is to link up with the national communications network or satellite links to get the pictures and sound back to 'base'.

Location editing has become an important skill in home and foreign news stories. With the development of satellite communications and lightweight portable editing packs, picture and sound editors can travel with their equipment and set up wherever electricity supplies allow. Portable satellite ground stations, carried in a couple of suitcases, can send stories back directly to the studio.

MIKE'S WISE WORDS – 29

Why is the television control room called a gallery? I'm told it stems from the early days of BBC Television News, which used to be produced in part of a building in London known as Alexandra Palace, which previously had been used for many purposes including displaying paintings. The news would be produced on the ground floor, which was next to the studio, but the control room was on the next floor which could only be accessed by mounting the stairs to the picture gallery running around the inside of the building. Moving to the control room used to be known as 'going to the gallery'.

Broadcast or Print?

It is not unknown for journalists to 'cross the tracks' either from newspapers into broadcasting or vice versa, but there are some differences between the two forms of journalism. I generally feel that newspaper journalists have an easier time of it, since they don't necessarily have to justify everything they write. It's much easier, as a print journalist, to ring someone up and get them to confirm a few points and give you a quote to confirm a (sometimes) pre-written story. A broadcast journalist actually has to get someone to say the words 'on air' in order to support a story – and it does mean that sometimes a television or radio story falls down because of a lack of supporting evidence!

On the other hand, people are often far more beguiled by a microphone or camera, and are ready to talk about the most amazingly personal things in front of millions of viewers. However, the sight of a newspaper reporter writing something down in a notebook, and then seeing their own words in print without tone, emphasis or inflection, can sometimes scare the pants off people.

MIKE'S WISE WORDS – 30

Some politicians, fed up with being quoted 'out of context', as they see it, have taken to recording any interviews conducted with the media, so that they have ammunition if the material appears to be 'misused' in print or on television! One well-known politician actually asks broadcast journalists how much time they have 'on air' for an interview. When you tell him, say three minutes, he takes a stopwatch out of his pocket and sets it off when you ask your first question. After exactly three minutes, he will just stop talking – all designed to prevent you from cutting his interview about!

Using the Print Journalism Route

The route you take is up to you. Newspapers are much more a medium of record, broadcasting is a more immediate, but transient, platform. People with 'ink in their veins' have a healthy contempt for their colleagues in the broadcast area with their make-up bags and Armani flak jackets ... the broadcasters often prey on more intensively staffed newspapers for their stories.

Newspapers are constrained only by self-imposed rules, supported by an industry-elected group of their peers, whereas in the UK broadcasters find themselves subject to control by a government-appointed body. Opinions can be much more readily expressed by print journalists, whereas a broadcast journalist is bound by 'the **guidelines**' to be as impartial as possible (with a few special exceptions, which are carefully controlled).

THE PROFESSIONAL'S VIEW – LOWRI TURNER

Lowri Turner is well known to viewers of a number of BBC television programmes, in addition to being a presenter/guest on talk shows where opinion matters. She started as a journalist and worked her way up to be fashion editor of the London *Evening Standard*, which is when she started being courted by the small screen.

I think you need to be calm to get on with people. Enjoy talking to real people, there is a major fashion for the public being on screen now so it is important to be able to speak with them, not just sit around in celebrity locations.

I know I'm biased because I came to TV presenting through journalism, but I think it has a huge advantage. Journalists are trained to interview people and are used to making people feel comfortable, to gain their trust.

> Lowri has very strong opinions – which make her a great guest. One of the areas she feels strongly about is TV presenting courses. 'I don't know anyone on screen who has done a TV presenting course. My advice is don't waste your money. You either have some talent or you don't, it's not something you can learn.'
>
> She feels strongly about using the journalistic route into broadcasting:
>
> > Unless you are incredibly good looking like a model or you have a talent for comedy and would fit into children's programming, I would recommend going into journalism and specializing in a particular area. It gets you noticed and, once you start guesting on other people's programmes, you also get thought about as a presenter in your own right.

A lot of people I know have progressed from work experience at local newspaper and/or local radio level, to full-time work and then on to regional television newsrooms, jumping to national programmes. There is a 'pecking order', and a healthy contempt all the way up and down that ladder as well!

How to Start

Most TV journalists start behind the scenes as researchers or news writers in the newsroom. They will try to find items, check the accuracy of stories given to them and write news bulletins. They may graduate from there to reporter level and be sent out with a camera operator or crew to cover local events.

Journalists on local stations will report on local hospital bed shortages, visits by politicians, football hooligans, the first new babies of the year, etc. Reporters only have a couple of hours to put together a story and decide how it should be presented. There may be a couple of interviews with local people followed by a **piece to camera** (PTC) giving the background information and reviewing the situation.

The job requires intelligence, quick wittedness and an ability to get along with other people. The ambition of local reporters is to graduate to national news or to a prestigious current affairs programme such as *Newsnight*. These news shows also have correspondents who report from all over the world, or have a specialist responsibility like social affairs, parliament or showbiz.

Newscasting

Newsreaders and newscasters have the most glamorous jobs and can be very highly paid. They must have a pleasant appearance, good diction, a comfortable manner and be able to remain calm when chaos is breaking out all around them. Some newscasters are experienced journalists and write their own copy, but many have their scripts prepared for them by back-room journalists in the newsroom. (Their colleagues out on the road sometimes have thinly veiled contempt for the skills of presenting, calling newscasters **autocue pilots** or **talking heads**.) News presenting is a particular skill and needs a lot more expertise than many people give credit for. The real talent for keeping cool shows up when everything starts to go wrong in the studio!

Whether you want to be the next Trevor McDonald or Walter Cronkite, or just shape public opinion as an elite faceless member of 'the media', there are a few hoops you have to jump through to start a career in the television news industry. True, working in TV news can beat working in a lot of other places; it's never dull, no two days are the same, and after two or three years you can earn good money. But in order to land that job, you'll have to start out doing some low-paying entry-level work – if you're lucky!

MIKE'S WISE WORDS – 31

Compared to being a network news presenter, most other jobs pale into insignificance. Think about it. These people work for maybe six hours a day, spend half an hour reading something somebody else wrote, get all the credit for it, and go home more famous than most politicians or actors. It's not fair! More to the point – you should be one of them!

Current Affairs, Factual and Documentary Programming

This area embraces enormous diversity: human-interest stories, science, history, biography and much more. The pure journalists in news used to 'look down' on their colleagues in the worlds of current affairs and documentaries. The thought was that these, rather more effete, journalists would spend too much time talking and 'reflecting' on the news and not enough time getting on with the job. Sometimes it would take – and still does – six months to a year for a programme to come to fruition. What did they do all that time? And, of course, the current affairs journalists always thought the news teams were far too brash and too quick to react.

Well, there's still a certain amount of abrasion between the two areas, but they actually can't do without each other. After the hard news has been **broken** there are large areas to be amplified and the work on looking at the background of news stories and investigative research are equally rewarding as being on the **front line**. The emphasis of such programmes is usually on research and production, and the jobs often favour people who are happy to spend long and painstaking hours on the telephone or in the library. In recruiting people for such jobs I have often taken into account the way in which a university education trains you to be very structured and rigorous in your research.

Skills Needed

The skills that you require for broadcast journalism are increasing. Not only do journalists write stories, they can now also edit them, thanks to technological developments. After filming – or videoing – an interview or report out in the field on **ENG** (Electronic News Gathering), a reporter could find themselves beaming the material back to base from a satellite truck – **SNG** – or taking the material back to edit themselves. Some stations are experimenting with self-operation news cameras, so that a reporter will film, edit, introduce and beam back all their material by themselves. Such multi-skilled individuals are sometimes called **VJs** (video jockeys).

Training

Journalism training which is specifically geared to television is less easy to find than general journalism training. Many people enter journalism through BBC or independent local radio, which provides excellent experience. The big news organizations also have a relatively small number of traineeships, which are sometimes advertised. A number of reputable courses, which include radio and television as part of the curriculum, are listed in Chapter 14.

Most people in broadcast journalism are graduates. At present, many entered the profession after gaining a first degree in a subject of their choice followed by a postgraduate broadcast journalism course. However, degrees in journalism are now increasingly available and are gaining **BJTC** recognition. Some are devoted specifically to broadcasting, others cover more than one journalistic discipline. There are also training schemes run by the BBC, ITN, Channel 4 and other companies. Again, a first degree is generally necessary to gain a place. Some postgraduate courses will accept people, especially mature applicants, who do not have a degree but who have relevant work experience and can demonstrate a commitment to a career in broadcasting.

The majority of trainees are recruited into the industry after attending vocational training courses for graduates. If you are absolutely serious about making a full time and successful career in broadcasting, the only certain way to do it is to go to a good university and emerge with a good grade and a fistful of work experience. However, for those who cannot follow this ideal route, it is worth giving a vocational college course a shot. Courses are held at colleges and universities accredited by the **NCTJ**. Some of these are for graduates only; others require five GCSEs including English, and two A-levels. This route is known as pre-entry.

You can apply for a college course through the NCTJ. Send for an application form to the National Council for the Training of Journalists, enclosing an A4 stamped addressed envelope. If they like your application, you will need to take a written test and if you succeed at this, you will be interviewed at a college of their choice. Some colleges have fast track courses; many colleges will only grant places if the applicants have already been on a brief work experience placement at a newspaper.

Staking Your Claim to be a News Presenter

Accumulate tapes of your work as evidence of how you come across on the air, and put together a **showreel** to be sent on request to stations where you apply for a job, see pages 72–4 and 84–7. Reports from the scene, especially live feeds, reveal the most about your potential as a reporter. Include a sample of your newscasting too, since it can indicate potential, but don't put it at the start of your tape. If the news director is looking for a reporter, what counts most is how well you report from a news scene.

Even if you have no tapes of stories used on the air, you can still record examples of how you perform as a reporter and newscaster. Just note for the prospective employer that they are pilot examples, not real. Skip gimmicks such as using part of the tape to tell the news director how great you are – your work should speak for itself.

Make multiple copies of your audio or video showreel. A few stations may want to keep yours on file for future consideration. If you want the tape back when it's not required, you might have to enclose a stamped, self-addressed envelope. I get dozens of tapes from hopefuls every week, and if I had to send them all back at my own expense, I'd need a second mortgage.

Heading Up the Ladder

The first step is usually to prove yourself as a reporter. If you come across well on the air, you may get to do some daytime or weekend anchoring – step two. As you develop, your primary job may become anchoring instead of reporting. And this third step will probably mean a good boost in pay. But you must work up to it. If you want to go on the air as a presenter right away, your best bet is radio news in a small or medium market.

Unless you work strictly behind the scenes, your voice and appearance must be acceptable for interviews and on-the-spot reports. While golden voices and glamorous faces are not required, you need to communicate clearly, credibly and pleasingly. Broadcast reporters not only cover the news, but must be able to tell it effectively into a microphone and, for television, a camera.

To target work in the regional TV newsroom it is essential to know the programmes well before you apply. Get a feel for the TV station to which you are applying. You will probably be asked your views on improving the programmes – what elements are missing, which features work best, etc.

The smaller the staff, the greater the variety of things you're likely to do. Look at it, too, as an opportunity to try out positions to see which fit best for your later specialization. Most reporters at the station level are on general assignment and thus regularly cover all kinds of news. But, mainly in large operations, there are specialists in such areas as business, consumer affairs and health. Veteran specialist reporters and news anchors tend to be among the best paid.

Work Experience

I run through the importance and value of work experience in Chapters 1 and 12, but with news there are certain extra things you need to think about when applying to the newsroom. The best way to begin your journey to the anchor desk or editor's chair is with some work experience. Getting a first-hand peep into the guts of a newsroom can tell you whether you want to work full time in a world where people swear at each other for no reason and never get any sleep.

Live television is a place where deadlines aren't flexible, so any newsroom can develop a crisis atmosphere in a flash. The more crises there are, the more chances you have to be a hero. Try to spot little things that need to be done and do them. If you catch a factual error in a script, say so. If you hear a phone ringing and nobody can get to it, pick it up. (And then say something into it!)

MIKE'S WISE WORDS – 32

Always keep your passport on you, no matter what level you're working at in a newsroom. It's a rule that I've always observed, and twice when I was working in a newsroom it led to me being

---

> sent off on a foreign breaking story. The story breaks overseas, the Editor strides into the newsroom asking 'Anyone here got their passport?' and if that's you, you could find yourself heading for the airport on a major international story. It happened to me during the Turkish invasion of Cyprus, and once when a plane crashed into the Bois de Boulogne near Paris. I'm not saying it turned me into a broadcasting star, but having my passport certainly kept me near the centre of the action, and the experience I gained was terrific

There are two career **tracks** in TV news: production and on-air. The production track involves working your way up to being a producer. Producers are responsible for putting together coverage and building it into a story. Whether it is an entire show or a taped piece that a reporter narrates, producers look after the building blocks to any news programme. They often start as production journalists, fast-forwarding through hours of archive footage to find the right shots. The next step is being an associate producer, which usually means fast-forwarding through more tape archives, until you become a producer.

If you want to be an on-air reporter quickly, your best bet is a local station in a small market. If you want to be an award-winning producer for *Newsnight*, you probably want to pursue an entry-level job at a network station. But if your desire for mad cash takes a back seat to your yearning for small-town fame, it's not unheard of for recent graduates to be offered jobs as reporters at small stations straight out of university.

How to Apply for Work Experience

Call the newsroom of your chosen company and ask for the work experience co-ordinator – most big TV and radio stations, as well as newspaper offices, have one, and a name and address of the specific person who accepts work experience applications will do. Newsrooms can be busy, scary places, so this initial call is not the time to spill your ambitions about how you want to give voices to the voiceless through the powerful medium of broadcast journalism. If you sense that the person is not in a hurry, maybe say who you are and where you are being educated, but do not try to turn a cold call into an interview.

Get a specific name and make sure you have the correct spelling. Errors can kill any covering letter in any job application, but in journalism they take on a special meaning. Even in television, part of your pay comes from the fact that you spell things correctly. Send a letter filled with spelling errors to a traditional company and they'll just think you're an idiot. Send one to a TV newsperson and they'll picture their newscast filled with butchered vocabulary on the day you 'help out' in the graphics department. Send off your stuff, and if you don't hear back in a week, then call. Journalists will respect you if you are persistent and show an ability to get people on the phone without being too annoying. That's because their jobs involve being persistent, getting people on the phone, without being too annoying...

You should write to a number of companies, explain why you think you would make a good reporter and ask if they will allow you to join their team for a few days. Try to pick a time other than June or July, when pressure on work experience places is at its greatest.

Other Opportunities

There are **news agencies** across the country that take on trainees. Agencies do not tend to publish or broadcast reports, but sell stories and pictures to organizations that do. There are also journalistic opportunities in public relations. Most organisations have **PR** departments and these people may need to have similar journalism skills to those I have outlined. There may be a house journal, **press releases** or internal leaflets to write. The Institute of Public Relations (see Chapter 14) can send you details of work within their industry. When you do start sending out CVs, the routine is pretty much the same as when you found your work experience: get the specific name of the person to whom you should send your material, and follow up after a week. Just like in any job, blind mailings with generic greetings probably won't get you very far. If you send showreels, make sure to follow strictly whatever guidelines are listed in the job ad. When you do get that first call back, treat it like a hot story. Follow up quickly and do your homework.

The Job Interview

Know what's 'going on in the world', and the day's top stories. Be prepared to discuss three or four stories you have been following over the last few weeks. If you haven't been following any, do a little background reading. If the interviewer asks you what you think about any of the stories, don't give your personal opinion. Show that you can be objective. Talk about how the media has covered these issues and what you would do differently. (You can find more details on job interviews in Chapter 13.)

If you're heading to a local station, make sure you have digested the area papers before you walk into your meeting. If you're going to a network, don't walk inside without having read fully the *Daily Mail*, *The Times*, *Telegraph* and *Guardian* (especially on Mondays). Listen to the radio on the way. Being able to discuss the story of the hour with your interviewer shows them that you'll be up-to-the-minute on the job.

Do not be late. Have you ever seen an evening newscast where the presenter is still getting dressed or making notes to himself, or humming weird tunes for the first four minutes of the show? (If you have, please, send me a tape.) Deadlines aren't flexible in live TV. Strolling in late for an interview shows that you think they are.

Bring writing samples. Got any clips from your university news-paper? Bring them. (If you don't, and you are still in college, try to get some under your belt.) Otherwise, a good exercise is to grab some copy from the papers or the news wires – Associated Press, Reuters, etc. – off the web and rewrite them as 30-second anchor **reads**. (A 'read' is when an anchor reads the whole story into the camera, without introducing a reporter who delivers a live report or taped piece.)

Bring story proposals. Here's where you can blow your interviewer away. Research two stories that have been simmering on the back pages but which nobody is talking about. Or look into stories that everybody is talking about but nobody is writing about. Craft a brief proposal for each (a few paragraphs will do), saying why it's impor-tant, who you would talk to, and what footage you would show with it. These should not begin with 'Call the Prime Minister and ask him what he thinks about China.' If you're at a network they will already have this covered, and if you're at a local station they'll probably recommend you apply to their Beijing bureau. If done right, story proposals will almost always put you in a category above everyone else applying for the same job.

Be Prepared for Breaking News

Most ordinary firms probably won't make you stand around for 45 minutes if the local mayor resigns or there is a bank robbery at the other end of the region. In TV news, they might. If this occurs and you happen to know something about whatever the story is, count your lucky stars and speak up. Volunteer whatever information or sources you know about without getting in the way. Whatever you do, don't just sit there for a few minutes and then say you have to leave. Showing that you understand the nature of breaking news can be a nice plus for you right away.

Television news is a medium dominated by producers, so you need to 'produce' your interview, and not just show up at it.

MIKE'S WISE WORDS – 33

To convince an editor you are worth appointing you will need to be able to demonstrate the following:

- An interest in current affairs at all levels.
- A lively interest in people, places and events.
- An appreciation of the part a local TV station/radio station/ newspaper plays in the community.
- An ability to write in a style that is easy to understand.
- Good spelling, punctuation and grammar.
- An ability to work under pressure to meet deadlines.
- Determination and persistence.
- A willingness to accept irregular hours.

Photography

Photojournalism, as the term implies, is a journalism-based skill with photography as its foundation. To succeed as a photojournalist you will need to develop natural news sense in tune with an ability to use a camera and ancillary equipment to the best advantage.

Features Journalism

A feature is a story which is not news. Feature journalists are often specialists in arts, travel or current affairs. Examples of feature items would be 'Five most popular holiday destinations for Britains' or 'Asthma now affects half of children in Britain'. Along with writing skills, specialist knowledge of the specific area is a must. You are unlikely to be asked for this skill in a newsroom, although a lot of news organizations are developing a features side to their operations. This area also encompasses the 'diarist' or 'showbiz reporter' **genre**. These people know all the minutiae relating to celebrities and other famous people, and they have permanent subscriptions to magazines like *Hello*! and *OK*! and other periodicals with exclamation marks after their names. They're avid film-goers and TV watchers – they know anyone who is anyone.

Features are sometimes incorporated into programmes that appear as predominantly news shows, such as *Trevor McDonald Tonight*. These programmes look into problems affecting the public which have been in the news. But they go into greater depth, be it on the dangers of plastic surgery or how the illegal drugs trade has affected our relations with the Far East. These programmes are research-rich and usually have more researchers and producers than news shows do.

Special Correspondents

This area covers diplomatic and political reporters, and foreign correspondents who go to trouble spots as news is breaking, say on the outbreak of war or the election of a new government. Other correspondents are stationed in prominent cities such as Washington and Johannesburg, to provide on-the-spot stories. Special skills include nerves of steel, love of travel, specialist knowledge of a relevant field such as politics and ... sensitivity.

Sport

This area comes under the same heading as broadcast journalism because it requires the same basic skills and qualifications, except you also need a burning enthusiasm for sport. Many sportsmen and women end their field and track careers by moving across into writing and broadcasting about it, but only the good ones survive.

As with the journalism we have described, you have to learn how to express yourself creatively, intelligently and knowledgeably to a tight deadline in sports journalism. Sport is a passionate hobby for many people, so knowing a lot about the teams you support may make you feel like you're already an expert and ready to have it out with Gary Lineker. You may be an expert on Manchester United or the All Blacks, but the people in this profession have to be experts on all the teams, in all the sports. It's hard work and part of that work is appearing on TV and acting like there is no effort in knowing as much about the runner-up in some basketball championship as you know about the hooker for Wasps. This can't be overstated: you have to know about more than your beloved football.

As with all broadcasting my first piece of advice would be to get a job at a newspaper, TV or radio station in any capacity. A job that involves writing and reporting will stand you in good stead. Once you are inside, you hear about job openings before anyone else does, and remember – tailor your showreel to be sports specific. Constantly update the tape as you improve. Also, listen to your own work and critique it.

Watch, or listen to, the people who are doing the job that you want to do one day. Figure out how you will fit into that show. What would you do differently? What do you like? What do you not like? In any event, you'll blow your audition or interview if you have not done your homework on the show you are trying out for.

One of the problems with sports broadcasting in particular is that people see the likes of Des Lynam or Jim Rosenthal and they think they can do it. People don't watch *The West Wing* and think they can be President, it's more difficult than it seems – we know that! But people watch Gary Lineker host the World Cup, or Tony Adamson do a golf tournament, and they reckon 'That's a great job. I could do that. I know as much as those guys. I say the same thing down the pub with my mates!' It isn't that easy. You need to be an expert, get five or six sports under your belt that you know in depth, and have a further five that you know all about. There should be no sport played anywhere that you don't understand.

So What Do We Know Now?

- *News is a 'must carry' element of many television networks – you should never be out of a job*
- *Journalist qualifications are absolutely necessary in newsrooms*
- *Hours can be very unsociable, but exciting*
- *Print journalism is a good way into the broadcast business*
- *You can also get into current affairs and documentaries*
- *Always keep your passport on you!*
- *The ability to write clearly and understandably is a must*
- *Sports broadcasters must know about all sports*

Jobs

CHAPTER 9

Jobs in Television

It takes a large number of people to keep a television station on the air. Many people on the outside of the business only ever see the faces that appear on the screen and there are a (small) number of little old ladies on the south coast who still believe that the presenters do everything! It may be that the areas of presentation and production that take up the larger part of this book are not the ones that interest you. Here, then, is an exhaustive A–Z of the sort of jobs that are needed in front of and behind the camera. Even if you only intend to do news reporting, it helps to know how many other disciplines there are in the station.

Jobs, positions, titles and their combinations vary from station to station. Keeping in mind that the same person may serve as two or more of the following, here are some of the people or positions.

Accounting

Accountant, Assistant Accountant, Auditor, Payroll
All these jobs are vital to the business of television – especially if you want to get paid! People with accounting backgrounds have been known to use this as a route to get into the production side of the business. There's a well-known cricket correspondent who started this way – at least he's never likely to get his match statistics wrong.

Acting

Actors, Choreographers, Dancers, Puppeteers, Singers, Voiceover Artists
Most of these jobs are done on a totally **freelance** basis and you

would need to develop your skills in another area before offering them to television. Of the list above, only the voiceover artist and actors on soaps would be in regular employment.

Administration

Secretarial, Administrators, Human Resources
The majority of secretarial staff have completed a course covering **IT skills** and office practice. A good telephone manner and the ability to assess priorities and deal tactfully with people are essential. There are various levels of secretaries in the BBC, ranging from junior secretary to senior executive Personal Assistants.

Administration opportunities vary, but the general requirements are excellent organizational and team-working ability, plus other skills depending upon the department concerned. For example, a financial area will require the ability to process data and information, therefore numeracy is essential, as well as the ability to operate computerized systems. In the production areas, computer literacy is required, plus an interest in the **programme output**.

Your first job will probably cover more than one. You may report, shoot video, produce the TV package and do a web version all on the same story. **Multiple duty** assignments, long common in small markets, are now a trend in markets of all sizes. Versatility and flexibility are key to getting a job and developing your talents. The more things you can do, the better.

Agents
Agents are employed by presenters, actors, singers, etc. to do deals with television companies. Therefore, they generally only represent people that TV companies would want to employ. However, some companies do employ agents in consultancy roles and also use former agents as 'talent managers' to help 'massage' the egos of the main on-screen performers and keep them loyal to their station. If you want to work as an agent, you will have to start as a junior at one of the big talent agencies, mainly based in London, that look after television and film performers. Most agents develop their own **client list** and earn their money by taking *a commission* or percentage (15 per cent is a usual fee) from their particular clients' earnings. (See Do I Need an Agent?, pages 59–60.)

Animation

Animator, Digital Artist, Optical Camera Operator

This area deals with special effects and the employees normally originate from art schools and colleges. Only a few broadcasters (the big ones!) can afford to employ staff animators or camera operators – it's a specialist service normally hired for particular productions. However, many graphics operations have switched over to digital, and graphic artists who formerly worked with paper, cardboard and paint now use electronic paint boxes. The competition for working in the graphic design area is high, as it often involves a move to set design and model making.

Artist Management

See also *Agents*. Most on-screen presenter/performers are recruited and looked after within each production by the executive producer or producer. For drama productions, casting directors are used, and these specialist individuals usually work as freelances, supplying their services to a wide number of different productions. They keep large quantities of photos and tapes cataloguing the skills and **cast types** of thousands of individuals.

Business Managers

The industry is now heavily loaded with people who calculate and monitor the running costs of all productions. Some are skilled producers, some come from accountancy or legal professions, others come direct from business school. Since the broadcast industry in Britain became a serious profit-making business rather than a pleasant plaything for already rich individuals, the business managers have seen their career ladder shoot through the ceiling!

Cameras

Camera Operators, Assistant Camera Operators, Specialist Camera Operators, Teleprompt Operators, Electronic News Gathers, etc.

This category covers a wide multitude of disciplines. Studio camera people are obviously highly skilled and usually work in teams with a senior cameraperson as **shift leader**. The job develops through trainee and assistant levels, with the junior members often responsible for moving the camera cables silently and safely around the studio as the cameras change position. The cameraperson is linked to the production gallery by headphones and encouraged by the director, who will call up each shot from those offered by the individual cameras in the studio. Although the casual outsider will see cameras as being under permanent 'instruction', in fact camerapersons are often left very much to suggest and offer good **shots** to the gallery. **Outside broadcast** cameras are also highly skilled, and sports occasions can be made or marred by the reactions of camera people. Good camera operators can second-guess the needs of the director, and watching a team of cameras cover a football match can be very instructive.

ENG camera operators carry their own recording equipment, either as part of the camera or slung over their shoulder. Again, a smart camera operator will now go into automatic operation at the scene of a major news story and will need little instruction from a director or reporter. Other specialist camera work includes **Steadicam** operation, a device which smooths out pictures in unsteady environments like cars, helicopters or crowds, and underwater camera work. Camera jobs are developed through traineeships and college work.

Teleprompters and autocue operators come into this section, as their equipment is often attached to the cameras. The main skills needed here are good keyboard skills and a patient temperament (for dealing with presenters and directors in tense moments). Much of this work is done on a freelance basis and can be easily learned if you can type.

Casting

Casting Directors, Casting Assistants

See also *Artist Management*. Casting directors are extremely powerful people but, rather like barristers in the legal world, they rely on their colleagues in the industry to feed them work – which leads to a Catch 22 situation: you've got to work as a casting director to get a reputation, but you have to have a reputation before you get work. Most casting directors start out as assistants to other casting directors and the magic wand gets handed down from generation to generation. As illustrated earlier in this A–Z, a casting director hoards details of all different kinds of performers so that when they need to cast a one-legged, Irish speaking, blonde female, they can take one straight out of their contacts book! Get your name listed by a casting director and the work could start to flow in. Become an assistant to a casting director and you're on the ladder to power!

Catering

Yup, people in television actually eat just like us ordinary mortals! There are some amazing companies around who service television and film companies on location and at their headquarters. The business has been used by some to get noticed as potential TV or film stars – and if you go to Hollywood every other waiter or waitress in the restaurants around LA is a star-in-waiting! If you don't fancy the television production route, this is an excellent way of hanging around the **A list** set. Catering students are the best potential recruits but, if you make a good sandwich, it could be a great way of taking a peep at how the TV people live.

Some television companies have people who look after all the catering requirements of their staff and their productions without ever picking up a butter knife in anger. It's all part of television management.

Construction

Set Construction, Carpenter, Scene Painter, Model Maker, Propmaker, Blacksmith, Welder

See also *Set Decoration*. These jobs are all to do with **set** building, although again the work is often put out to freelance or self-employed people. There's a real technique to making a bit of wood and canvas look like the real thing, and often it helps to have something of a design-student background so that you can guarantee the authentic look of the scenery you build. Not only must it all be put together to look like the real thing, but in studios where time is of the essence and your production of *Richard III* is being followed by *Wheel of Fortune*, it's all got to be capable of quick construction and **striking**.

Nearly all new designs have models made so that a production team can see how easy the set is going to be to move around, and make last minute adjustments before giving the real thing the green light. Some set models are so intricate that they can be sold for quite a price after they've been used.

Props are also an interesting area, and if they have to be specially and authentically made, it requires quite a skilful individual to build the items required. Often, prop and set makers will have to make several versions of the same item because the plot calls for a large explosion or fire!

Blacksmiths are needed for all sorts of complicated ironwork that both decorates the set and supports it with special struts and girders.

Design

Set Designer, Set Dresser, Graphics Designer, Graphics Assistant, Caption Generator Operator

The design department in television covers all the areas that derive from the art college design courses, even though some of the jobs are now done totally through electronics rather than through paint and paper. The set designer creates all sorts of television scenery and backdrops, and will also be something of a **location expert** as well. Set design not only involves the skill of creating authentic scenery but knowing how the lighting will work, and how cameras and performers will move in, out and around the designed set. Once the set is built, the set dresser or stylist will attend to making sure that the set looks the same every day and is kept up-to-date. The graphics designer will be responsible for all sorts of on-screen animations and captioning. They will often also design the title sequences for programmes and have them filmed specially. Many programmes need caption generator operators, who will set up banks of captions which will run across the bottom of the screen, giving people's names or additional information relevant to the programme.

Directors

Directors, Assistant Directors
   The director is the person who is in charge of putting the actual show to air or onto tape. He or she co-ordinates the whole technical 'realization' of any production and sits in the production gallery keeping everything going, calling the camera shots and encouraging the whole team – cameras, sound, floor staff, production assistant, vision mixer and performers – to give of their best. It's a nerve-wracking and often lonely job. Directors in some areas of news production get so worn down that they have special agreements allowing them to retire at 40, and maybe move into a more gentle area at lower pay.
   Assistant directors will often work in a smaller area (or sub-gallery), producing elements of a programme that will feed into the main gallery and become part of the overall output.
   Outside the studio, directors will look after outside broadcasts and will also direct small films that can be recorded and edited ready for dropping into larger programmes – for instance, a programme dealing with a Grand Prix motor race might have specially shot 'profiles' of all the drivers which were made during the weeks leading up to the actual race. These smaller films will be called inserts – they still have to be produced and directed.
   The route to becoming a director is either via art college and/or film school, or by joining a programme as a runner, becoming a researcher and then graduating to AP – assistant producer. APs are often used as trainee directors, making small insert films and directing segments of

programmes. It's often at the AP stage that people make a decision as to whether their career is going via the editorial producer direction or the more technical director route.

Aspiring directors often have a good eye for **picture construction** and are very sharp in spotting how a picture can be shaped for the television screen.

Many of the larger broadcasters run courses for people who want to travel the director road, and will then arrange for you to be attached to programmes that can gradually put you to work.

Editing

Film Editor, Video Picture Editor, Music and Sound Editor

The editor works in the area of television known mainly as 'post **production**'. The film or video has been shot and the music recorded, but the material needs to be put in the right order and made to flow seamlessly so that it tells a story in picture and sound. Film editors still get their hands dirty on the actual material although they view the film on special machines, usually a **Steinbeck**. A film needs 24 frames of picture for each second and the skilled film editor can hold the transparency up to the light and choose exactly which frame to cut and join on to the next sequence. The separated pieces of film are glued together to make one complete negative from which a master, **positive copy** is produced for **transmission**.

A relatively new technique in film editing is to transfer all of the film onto video and then put the result through a video-editing process instead. This begs the question why shoot on film? The practitioners will assert that material shot on film has a greater **picture depth** than electronic material. However, the video people will tell you that they can now produce picture 'depth' at the flick of a switch! Don't bother arguing with anyone about this – you will never move the film people from their ideas about video and vice versa. Just nod.

Video editing came in with a vengeance in the late 1970s and several film editors were re-trained in the new art. Thankfully that meant that artistic picture construction didn't go totally out of the window, and video editing has become as skilful as its cinematic elder sibling. Filming on video (the word film has stuck, even though the picture is electronically constructed) started mainly in the news field, where speed was essential. But it has spread to all sorts of areas, including the most complicated of drama programming.

Sport is also an area that has benefited enormously from video work, with instant action replays and beautifully **constructed montages** (clips of video skilfully edited together, often set to music).

The same skills can be used in editing music and sound generally in order to enhance a visual production. Sound engineers can spend hours getting the music or the effects just right to make a mundane picture become very eerie or exciting. With computerization, the razor blades and tape of yesterday have disappeared, in favour of the visual sound editing system.

There is a well tried route into all of these jobs, as an assistant to someone who has already accumulated the skills. If you have prepared the way with a college course first, you will be a prime candidate.

Electrics/Lighting

Lighting Designer, Lighting Director, Technician, Gaffer
The business uses electricity to function, so the requirements for an electrician are pretty obvious. The union grip on the business has been relaxed now, but once it was not possible to switch a light on or change a bulb in a studio without an electrician being present, usually at quite a handsome fee. Electricians are, however, still a very necessary part of the business, whether in the studio or on the road.

Television productions can be made or ruined by being badly lit, which is why the skills of a television lighting designer and lighting director have rightly become more recognized. A good lighting director can iron out all sorts of problems with a set or a performer. Top actors and actresses know the value of the person who lights them well and makes wrinkles and surplus flesh disappear, and the lighting director is often the first person they want to make friends with before entering a studio.

All of these jobs are approached through the route of apprenticeship and certficated courses.

Hair and Make-up

Hair Stylist, Make-up Artist, Prosthetics Artist
With the advent of more sophisticated electronic cameras, the need for heavy make-up in ordinary programmes has begun to recede. However, the skill of the make-up artist and hair stylist continues strongly with productions in drama, some more studio-based operations, game shows and entertainment programmes. In some dramas, the hair stylist will produce the goods without anyone present, by the use of wigs, etc.

Many companies now provide all performers with their own make-up kit, and the make-up artist or designer is used as a consultant to advise performers on how to use the material on themselves.

Both the hair and make-up roles have an added dimension, which directors and producers have long recognized – that of counsellors. The chance to take a break in the make-up room chair and talk about problems, whether about work or life in general, is a very therapeutic one and can often be used as an opportunity to iron out little local difficulties on a production. More than one Hollywood star – and quite a few television performers – have ended up with a partner who did their hair or make-up!

A good training ground for hair and make-up is, obviously, on the job at a high street salon, or via the many college courses that are now available.

The prosthetics area – making extra body parts to be stuck on or worn as part of a costume – is obviously a skill picked up over several years, often by people who work with the disabled making artificial limbs and suchlike. In television or film, the mouldings are often done in rubber or a form of plasticine, and then coated with make-up to disguise the extra bit.

Locations

Location Director, Location Finder, Location Manager

How do you think they find the beautiful scenic backdrops to some of television's major successful series? Location directors are people who have amazing contact books full of photos of the weirdest places where filming can take place. Think of films like *Harry Potter*, where magic castles like Hogwarts and secret villages like Hogsmead needed to be built around existing locations (although much was reconstructed in the studio as well). Dozens of different locations were selected for each of the scenes, although in the completed film they look just like one complete place. The Hogwarts dining hall and some of the cloister scenes, for instance, were filmed at Christ Church college in Oxford – although when they finally got round to it, they needed to move windows up to make everyone look smaller, which after 500 years' untouched architecture was a bit much for the college authorities, so the producers ended up making an exact replica at the studios in Hertfordshire.

Music

Music Producer, Composers, Musicians, Singers, Groups and Bands

Most music produced for television comes from freelance composers and musicians and/or library music discs. Only a small amount of programmes will actually use staff composers and musicians. These roles will normally be filled by people hired in especially for the programme. There are a number of television companies who have specialist music producers on board: these are usually concerned with broadcasting live concerts or arts programmes. Obviously, a specialist knowledge of music helps, and music graduates are virtually the only people who would be eligible for these jobs.

News

News Editor, Chief Sub-editor, Sub-editors General Reporters, Specialist Reporters, Correspondents
This is dealt with in more detail in Chapter 8.

The news editor is the key person of the news team, taking control of a number of **bulletins**, deciding what stays in and what comes out and the order in which stories appear. The news editor is the one in overall control of the news department, responsible for overall decisions on style, news values, etc. There will be an assistant editor, who will assist with things like checking the **wires** and watching other news shows, to find out what's going on, what's old and what's new. A chief sub-editor will work with the news editor to check reports handed in by reporters, researches and journalists.

Other stories will have **news images** added in – video footage sent down the wires or from a freelance camera operator. Or they may be stills of people involved in the report, or digital pictures. The images are fed into the report while the newsreader carries on reading.

Reporters often specialize in a particular field such as sport, foreign affairs or health. In general they cover news stories, usually on-camera or tape and from the scene or the newsroom. Reporters develop sources by acting as researchers and interview **news makers**: those involved with the news story. They also gather information from **wire services** periodicals and computerized databases. Then they tell the story with words, sound and in television pictures. They often report live from the news scene without a script or even notes. Some reporters also become newsreaders, having worked their way up through the ranks of reporters.

Post Production

Post Production Supervisor, Dubbing, Video Recording
See also *Editing*. Once a programme has been put together in a studio or on film, it may very well need to be post-produced, or be altered in a specialist post-production suite. The addition of music and sound effects, or commentary, after editing is a highly skilled

affair, but one which can be learned on the job. The dubbing suite and post-production jobs often come out of the sound department.

Presenting

Presenting, Announcing, Newsreading, Weather Forecasting
This is also dealt with in more detail, in Chapters 5–8).

The presenter is the person who fronts the programme and hosts guests for the viewers at home. This is a highly prestigious job and presenters get paid very well for what they do. There are no rules about how you can become a TV presenter, and there are no rules about how the presenter should do the job. Former newspaper journalists sometimes front serious political programmes. Light entertainment shows are often presented by singers and comedians; well-known chefs and writers of cookery books often end up hosting cooking shows or cookery slots in magazine shows. Thus one clear way to become a TV presenter is to become an expert in your field first. Television presenters Jonathan Ross and Esther Rantzen started off as TV researchers. If this is the way you are considering entering presenting, be careful not to be too keen and flexible so you never get given a chance to do serious work. At the same time, beware that no one wants to take on somebody who plans to spend his or her whole time looking for another job.

An announcer makes **announcements** between programmes giving information on what programme is to follow and any important details or warnings. If the programme touches on sensitive issues or includes strobe lighting, the audience at home need to know to enable them to take suitable action. The announcer also reports if there is a technical problem such as a **transmission fault**, or a change in the advertised programming: their job is to keep the viewer up-to-date. A clear and authoritative voice is a prerequisite, as is the ability to work independently and write your own material. The job of the announcer is to provide a faceless voice. Announcers are selling programmes: what they say and the way they say it are important factors in the success of the programme which is to follow. If it sounds dull people may switch off. Also, like presenters of weather reports, announcers are also there to fill time – they have whatever time there is between programmes to say what they have time to say. They work from a soundproof room behind the scenes. The ability to work independently, with attention to detail, is important.

News Presenter, Newscaster Anchor
This is a highly prestigious position with a great responsibility to the

audience to whom sometimes seriously bad news is given. It is not a job that comes easily and modern newsreaders are now chosen for their relaxed manner – authoritative but casual. The newsreader has to have perfect diction and clear delivery, and must not panic under pressure. Newsreaders are often faced with changes in running order and script at a moment's notice, but the viewer must never know this. The newsreader also acts as the on-air co-ordinator of a news programme. As both host and reporter, the newsreader reads news stories, introduces reports by others and may interview **news sources** live. They have the skills to weave the programme together for listeners and viewers. A newsreader may also serve as a programme's managing editor or producer, and may report from the scene of news events. News, sports and weather anchors interact as a team.

Weather presenting is an interesting job. It is not necessary to have meteorological knowledge, although the BBC's weather people are all skilled and the weather presenters on other channels have usually had at least a basic course in meteorology. For a number of stations, the weather presenter is the third member of a presenting team after the main anchors. For this reason, the person will often be chosen for their personality, sense of humour and ability to think on their feet, and they add to the general gaiety and fun of a programme. People, especially children, feel more confident about writing to the weather presenter, who often presents a more human face than the news-readers. The straightforward weather presenters are used between programmes and often have to cope with sudden changes of timing when the programme before them has over-run.

Production

Producer, Executive Producer, Associate Producer, Line Producer, Producer's Assistant, Production Assistant, Production Manager, Production Secretary, Unit Manager

A good producer is incredibly organized and thorough when it comes to a particular story; all the facts have to be absolutely accurate, which goes without saying, but sometimes mistakes are made and that's when credibility can be lost. A good producer knows that he or she is the boss, but also works as a member of the team and recognizes team spirit in others. The producer picks the team, controls the budget and makes all the key decisions during production. To be a producer you must be a good manager, skilled at planning ahead, dealing with budgets, etc., which is where qualifications in the management of people or money come in handy. Experience in TV, such as in research or floor management, and a proven interest in making programmes are mandatory with the top producers. You are most likely to work up to becoming a producer through promotion as you learn about TV and production.

The executive producer is the overall supervisor of news producers and co-ordinator of production elements of news programs. They are often the chief producers of principal news programmes. They work with the news director on matters of programme format and content, and production financial, budget and personnel performance. Executive news producers often move up to become news directors.

The floor manager organizes and is responsible for everything that needs to be done in the studio on filming day. If there is an audience the floor manager will ensure everything goes smoothly with them, telling the audience when to clap or laugh, etc., and ensuring that no empty seats are seen on screen. They are also in charge of safety: studios are dangerous places – heavy equipment and high voltage cables are scattered around. The floor manager will inform the audience about any safety issues and keep an eye on the crew. They liaise with the director in the **gallery** who will pass information to the presenter via the floor manager, and will use sign language to instruct the presenter – on which camera to look into, etc.

The job of floor manager is also a step towards becoming a director because of all the studio equipment knowledge needed. Personal traits required are to be lively, have an open mind, and be bright, educated, full of ideas and enthusiasm and great with people. Prior experience in journalism helps – it shows you have experienced a fraught newsroom.

The floor manager mediates between the producer and director (both in the gallery) and the studio. They pass on instructions to the studio team and so tact is a useful skill! The floor manager is also responsible for overseeing the studio audience, so excellent communication and organizational skills, as well as a sound knowledge of technical and safety issues, are vital to this role.

Once you have your first job, if you do well, you will get offered more. To help ensure this, make as many contacts as you can – producers, production companies, other researchers. Once people know you are keen and friendly and want to make the effort, work will find its way to you. Write to everyone possible – most producers will keep good letters and CVs on file for future reference. If you nudge them every few months with an updated CV then you should remain in the back of people's minds, but do not pester.

The production manager's role is similar to the production assistant role, but the job involves much more responsibility, especially in the area of money and budgets which are becoming increasingly important as budgets get tighter and broadcasters become more demanding. You also have responsibility for general administration and the management of staff, both creative and operational. Good financial skills and managerial qualities are needed. A clear overview of the **production process** and understanding of the funding of television are vital. Production assistant is the most normal route in, but sometimes accountants are appointed. A production manager may go on to direct or produce but, more usually, would progress up the managerial path in a larger organization, such as the BBC, or on to Company Director in a small production company.

Property

Props Buyer, Prop Master, Props Assistant, Weapons Specialist
On the surface, looking after props might not sound the most stimulating job in the world, but it is quite an exacting and exciting role. First, there's the sourcing of material for all sorts of productions, from the mundane bottles of fake beer for a soap, to the finding of specific antique items for a period drama. It's almost like being a professional detective. Props buyers have minds like catalogues and are a bit like army quartermasters during a war. These jobs are scarce, but they do get advertised. Even more scarce is the weapons specialist role, which includes servicing and looking after guns and weaponry of all kinds – including swords and swashbucklers from way back when. For this job you really need to have been an armourer or similar in the armed forces!

Publicity/Marketing

Public Relations Officer, Press Officer, Listings Writer
Every television company needs someone to feed interesting stories about their programmes to the press and to offer pictures of performers and advance copies of programmes for critics to preview. A lot of creative writing takes place in the production of **listings** – details of the content of programmes that newspapers and magazines will print in advance so that viewers can decide what they are going to watch. Newspapers in the UK are relying more and more on stories about people who appear on television to fill their empty columns, and this hunger for stories needs feeding. Listings magazines are extremely popular, and also need constant streams of information about programmes.

Research

Researcher, Librarian, Copyright Clearance Assistant

The researcher's job allows you to be creative and make your mark on a programme. Research also has a routine and unglamorous side, and it is here that the successful researcher excels. Director General of the BBC, Greg Dyke, started off as a lowly TV researcher so, obviously, it's a good job to go for – and everyone knows it.

Being thorough, organized and knowing the facts of a story, and also having a bit of flair, all help to make a good researcher. Researchers are expected to do a wide variety of tasks such as going through the running order of the programme, checking scripts and querying things, finding good stories and ideas, and helping to set up the productions. They are most active in areas such as history, science and current affairs.

Researchers meet the public a lot and must be able to win people's confidence and put them completely at ease. You may be dealing with sensitive subjects. Take, for example, a programme on cancer; as a researcher on this programme you would need to know a little about cancer itself, as a disease, and, in a social context, what effect it has on sufferers. The people you would interview would either have lost a loved one to cancer or be about to lose themselves to it ... a potentially horrific situation, but riveting broadcasting. Getting a good interview would involve coaxing people along into telling their innermost feelings even though they are under terrific emotional pressure.

There are very few old researchers in TV. It is a young person's job and most researchers aim to become producers by the time they are 30. Broadcast research is different from academic research. As part of the production team, you would support the producer, contributing ideas, contacts and sources. You might select and interview possible contributors and write relevant material and briefings. The growth in new media has added significantly to the scope of a researcher's role. Before production starts, all topics must be researched, which demands accuracy and speed – scanning newspapers, reading press releases, using the Internet, etc. You are likely to have broadcasting experience or have worked as a journalist.

Librarians or archivists collect, collate and preserve information which might have been used or become useful in programmes. A specialist subject is useful, as is the ability to be organized and methodical, and IT database skills. Librarians in broadcasting often have to work at high speed to deliver material relevant to a broadcast that may be going out live, so a good, quick, memory is useful.

Scripting

Scriptwriter, Script Editor, Continuity Assistant

Whether it is creative writing, news scripts or documentary narratives, scriptwriting is a vocation, a job in itself, not something you expect to be 'promoted' up from. For news, journalists write news copy from information gathered from news services, network feeds, field reports, interviews, recordings and other sources. In most typical TV or radio operations, most writing is done by producers, reporters and anchors rather than by separate writers.

Where a production needs one, the writer is probably the most important creative link in the whole of the film and TV industries. In drama and comedy, writers hold the power to determine whether the show is a success or not. The scriptwriter needs to be a talented and entertaining writer and, in the case of soaps and drama, someone who has stories to tell. Scriptwriters decide on characters, their past, their future and what they say; they have to devise funny situations for comedy and cliff-hangers for soap operas or thrillers. On short or one-off series the scriptwriter will invent their characters and see them through to the end. On soaps the scriptwriter will be one of many, and will have to handle new characters invented by other writers. In documentaries the scriptwriter creates a **fact-based narrative** often spoken in **voiceover** form, guided by a series of pictures and, perhaps, interviews. It is quite likely in documentaries that the writer is also the producer or director.

There are many short courses in scriptwriting available at colleges as well as forming modules of media degrees. The main thing you need is proof that you can write and that you have ideas. If you have experience in journalism, in writing advertising copy or radio programmes, then it is clear that you are interested in writing and have proven success.

Sound

Sound Engineer, Sound Recordist, Audio Assistant, Boom Operator, Sound Effects Co-ordinator, Sound Editor

People always seem to believe that sound is far less important in television than the pictures. Not true. A good sound engineer can lend all sorts of dimensions to a television programme, and the best sound people are in great demand to add all the final gloss. The job entails not just handling microphones and making sure they're in the right places, but music and sound effects too. In a studio you would have a sound engineer and an assistant on the mixer in the control booth, and there would be sound assistants handling microphones on the studio floor, with boom mikes (crane-like devices which hover just out of sight over people's heads) or stick and radio mikes to place on desks and people's clothing. On location, there's at least one sound person on a single camera unit, handling recording and microphones – and on major outside broadcasts there could be many more, looking after things like crowd effects and insert interviews.

Special Effects

Pyrotechnician, Special Effects Co-ordinator
   These, of course, are very specialist jobs. You have to be something of a mad scientist to do them, or to even be interested in them. Pyrotechnics are not just fireworks, but include making guns go 'bang' and making people look as though they've been shot, with special exploding capsules that fix to the body. Special effects include all sorts of areas where people want strange things to happen. Sometimes you can achieve an effect electronically, other times you need to make it actually happen, like showing someone riding a horse and suddenly leaping into the air and flying, or playing Quidditch on broomsticks, and so on.

Stills Photography

If there isn't a stills photographer on the staff, there'll be one very close at hand to all television stations. Apart from the obvious need for publicity photographs, etc., there's also a need for skilled still photography in programme terms. Go into any designer's office and you'll find dozens of photographs pinned on the walls showing how a set is laid out, or how someone is dressed in a series, so that continuity is achieved by making sure everything looks the same next time filming takes place.

Stunts

Stunt Co-ordinator, Body Double, Fight Choreographer, Stunt Driver
   Similar to the special effects people. This is mainly film work, but because the edges between film and television are being blurred these days, with many TV companies also making cinema films, the work has crossed over between the two. Stunts and fights and driving scenes are now all part of a television studio's daily work. You can get yourself attached to someone who does such work on TV and films and learn how it's all done. A head stunt person will often be asked to bring several other people with them, to make up numbers. Good

luck with your insurance policies if you decide to take up this sort of work – and make sure you keep the first aid box handy.

Technical Engineer

The engineering side of TV requires a high level of ability. Broadcasting equipment has become more complex and sophisticated; engineers have to be well-qualified in electronic communications. Over 95 per cent of engineering entrants now have degrees. Most technical equipment in TV studios is maintained on site and the technical workshop can be permanently busy, repairing and upgrading equipment. Get yourself a good engineering degree and you'll never be out of work.

Transport

Drivers

Both on and off screen, no television company can do without drivers, whether it's to ferry the Chairman of the company to lunch, pick up an urgent news package, or demonstrate your skills in a car test. Guests on programmes, celebrities, etc., like to be well looked after, and often the first person they meet from a programme is the driver. The person at the wheel can put a star in a good mood on the journey to the studios and the whole production team can benefit. Like the make-up jobs, this role is often coupled with part-time counselling – drivers hear everyone's troubles and woes and the good ones can solve all sorts of problems, on the side!

Vision mixer

The vision mixer operates a **console** (or mixer) which controls what is on screen. This integrates effects and switches cameras to change the view on screen, and inserts pre-recorded material such as adverts. Instant reactions and good concentration are vital, because the vision mixer works to a timed script, often on live programmes. Good vision mixers often work as freelancers and are in great demand by directors who appreciate the speed and skill of vision mixers on top of their jobs. This is a good route to take if you want to become a director, and some studios actually let the director do their own vision mixing on shows. Although, like riding a bicycle, there are basic skills which you never forget, there is a constant need to update yourself as technical developments occur.

Wardrobe

This is a funny one, because many organizations have now done away with the need for wardrobe facilities on site and prefer to hire in costumes in the same way as many theatres do. Most presenter-led programmes provide the performers with a budget to buy their own clothing and have done away with the wardrobe role altogether. However, in companies where drama is a big part of the work there are wardrobe designers – and, of course, costumes to be made, cleaned and kept neat and tidy.

This is not intended to be an exhaustive list, but to give you something of an idea of the enormous variety of jobs available in the business. Some companies specialize in producing certain sorts of programmes, and they will structure their staff accordingly. Clearly, the accounts people won't get directly involved in making programmes, but they will feel part of the overall team and they get to see a lot of the people who do work on programme making – including the stars.

How the Jobs Work in The Studio

On the actual recording day the production crew will start by **blocking** the show; this means they'll sort out the different components of the show and how the cameras, sound and lighting will move around the various areas. On a chat show like *Jerry Springer* or *Trisha*, where guests move about on a stage, they will have to be coached through which door they must enter and exit, and which chair they must sit on. The show's researchers will do most of the organizing of guests after a briefing with the show's director.

The camera operators will take up their positions and get test shots whilst liaising with the studio electricians, who move and fix lights under direction from the lighting supervisor. The teleprompt people will type up and run through their scripted material with the presenter to make sure it's all correct, and make any changes needed.

The director and his team are stationed in the gallery, often above the studio, from where they can direct, observe and discuss what should happen on the **studio floor**. The gallery is usually divided into three sections: first, the central section, which contains the monitor screens showing what each camera is focused on, and which show what is being recorded and all the technical controls and communications systems linking the gallery to the studio. In this central section are the director, the producer, production assistant, vision mixer and technical operations manager, who is responsible for the technical quality of picture and sound. To the side of the central section is the lighting control with the supervisor, usually on the left. On the right side of the gallery is the sound supervisor and operator, ready to insert music or sound effects when required.

Once the guests are organized, the lighting correct and the director, producer and presenter satisfied, the final recording begins. As many people in the audience will not have been at a recording of a television show before, a warm-up person will often tell a few jokes and let the audience know what to expect. They will be encouraged to applaud new guests and laugh when appropriate. If there are commercial breaks they will be expected to applaud at the end and beginning of each new section of the show.

Most television companies run audience management offices and it's possible to get tickets for most live and recorded studio shows. As a start, it's a good idea to get yourself into an audience show and take a look around – just think, one day the audience might be filing into their seats and taking an envious look at you!

CHAPTER 10

Jobs in radio

Working in radio is a little different from TV. The teams are smaller so every role is vitally important to the running of a show. Whereas on TV the producer has a certain role and will handle a team of assistants and researchers and research assistants, in radio the producer will often research, write, produce and sometimes present as well. So prepare to be able to do everything in radio if you want to make a success of it!

It is important to realize that commercial radio companies are generally autonomous companies, which set their own standards when recruiting and training staff. These standards depend upon the market in which the station operates as well as local competition from other broadcasters. Stations are sometimes part of a larger group which operates a number of radio licences – the group may set recruitment standards or may leave the decision to local management. Your best bet is a direct approach to the station(s) you would like to work for.

Jobs, positions, titles and their combinations vary from station to station, so it is not as easy as in television to list specific job titles. Keeping in mind that the same person may serve as two or more of the following, here, in A–Z fashion, are some of the areas, people or positions.

Administration

Finance, Secretarial, Reception, Human Resources, Administration
Financial and administrative positions range from Accounts Clerk or Secretary to Company Secretary and/or Finance Director. Qualifications appropriate to the position will be required and range from

RSA bookkeeping or typing to a Business Studies degree or relevant professional qualifications. Remember that radio stations get hundreds of applications for each post they advertise and so will be looking for good qualifications but, above all, a flexible attitude and an enthusiasm for radio.

The majority of secretarial staff have completed a course covering IT skills and office practice. A good telephone manner and the ability to assess priorities and deal tactfully with people are essential. At the top level there is a great deal of responsibility and power, and it is possible to move up from the most lowly phone-answering, secretarial position to secretary to the Director General of the BBC.

Administration opportunities vary, but the general requirements are organizational and team-working abilities, plus skills specific to the job concerned. For example, a financial area will require the ability to process data and information and therefore numeracy is essential, as well as the ability to operate computerized systems. In the production areas, computer literacy is required, plus an interest in the **programme output**.

Accounting jobs are vital to the business of radio – especially if you want to get paid! People with accounting backgrounds have been known to use this as a route to get into the production side of the business.

Engineering

Technical Operator, Engineer
The technical operator or assistant is the backbone of the radio station; this is also a good way to start treading the path towards presenting because of the necessary understanding of how to operate the **desks**. Technical operators control the live on-air desk, which requires a cool head when faced with difficulties – such as guests walking out on the presenter before they have been interviewed. You might be required to cut to another tune or **jingle** to give the presenter time to sort something out. You will also get to work in the newsroom in this job, dealing with tape and stories.

Radio engineering covers everything from repairing and maintaining to operating equipment. Stations often recruit staff with an engineering degree or HND or a specialist qualification in electronics. Increasingly, stations are looking for people with good IT skills to manage a range of applications.

Management

Business, Programme, Editorial Management
The majority of managers in commercial radio have gained their positions after acquiring considerable experience within the industry. Few stations specifically recruit managers as such, and the majority of managing directors will have come up through the ranks and may have been programme controllers, news editors or sales managers.

The industry is heavily loaded with people who calculate and monitor the running costs of all productions. Some business managers are skilled producers; others come from accountancy or legal professions. Still others come direct from business school. Since the broadcast industry in Britain became a serious profit-making business rather than a pleasant plaything for already rich individuals, the business managers have seen their career ladder shoot through the ceiling!

Editors in radio are the same as newspaper and TV editors in that managerial skills are mandatory. In radio they develop, communicate and implement strategies for radio programmes and bulletins. Journalism skills are standard and a knowledge of radio production techniques, as well as a keen interest in news and current affairs, are required. Other skills needed are flexibility and understanding of the needs of a diverse radio audience, and a high level of organizational and communication skills. The need to manage and control the station's budget, making the most effective use of available resources, means experience of budgetary control is useful. Editors devise programme ideas and undertake various administrative duties. They take overall editorial responsibility for the standard, content and style of the station's programmes.

News

News Editor, Reporters
There is a differing number of jobs according to the stations involved. BBC radio has a very large news staff in London servicing all the network radio output, as well as material to regional and local radio. In addition to editorial desks for the seven national networks, there is a department known as GNS (General News Service), which receives copies of everything that comes into the whole corporation and re-sends it to departments that they think will be interested in a particular story. Teams of producers, editors and sub-editors work round the clock to feed the huge BBC machine. In local radio there are well-staffed newsrooms, which also feed material to the network

newsroom and to the region, as well as taking care – in some cases – of the needs of television. In commercial radio, the newsrooms are only staffed to a minimum level, often with only a news editor on day duty and two or three other staff who act as newsreaders and reporters on a rotational basis.

In local radio the newsreader or news reporters research and write their own news stories as well as reading them on air. It is usual for news reporters to have some experience in news journalism, although this is an area where media studies graduates often get their first job. Radio and TV journalism is often more about nerve and good communication skills than strict journalistic expertise. Ex-teachers are, in my experience, often among the best gatherers and tellers of news. Newspaper journalists sometimes find it hard to cross over to broadcast journalism because of the formulaic nature of newspaper writing, which gets in the way of telling the real story. There are, however, several possible pitfalls if you don't have a basic grounding in law and government matters – but a good newsroom boss should be there to protect you from making mistakes on air. It is also possible to attend college courses in the essential skills while working as a trainee in the newsroom.

You will be expected to know or learn how to use **portable audio recording equipment** and computer-based editing equipment to produce **packages** (news reports) for broadcast. The successful local radio reporter needs diligence and understanding as a journalist, a thorough knowledge of local, national and international news and current affairs and strong interpersonal skills. Career development usually follows one of two paths: news – starting as a reporter, moving on to become news editor; or programmes – starting perhaps as a researcher, and then becoming a producer, presenter or both. From there, many people move into management, or perhaps on to a role in a larger station. Local radio is still seen as an excellent training ground for those wanting to move eventually into television, though radio can still provide an interesting, exciting and rewarding career in its own right.

Presenting

DJ, Presenter, Continuity Announcer, Traffic and Weather Reporter

I go through presenting in great detail in Chapters 5–7. The job requires personality, an ability to talk and interview in an interesting manner and being able to operate studio equipment. Traditional routes into presentation work are through experience in hospital or college radio or DJing. Journalistic skills are very useful for interviewing people and chatting comfortably with your audience from the studio. If you have personality, ability and enthusiasm, stations may well offer training, and training courses are also available from third parties. The presenter in radio has to do a multitude of things, from **driving the desk**, cueing music and introducing news reports, to dealing with phone-ins and generally ensuring that the audience gets what they expect in terms of chirpiness and informality.

There are four 'on air' jobs in radio: the obvious one is the presenter/DJ. Presenters' backgrounds and experience vary; some experience is vital, but not everyone has a huge list of credits to their name before getting a foothold in radio presenting. A lot of presenting is done live and so requires a calm personality (a good sense of humour is useful) and an understanding of the uses of the technical equipment. The local radio presenter will also have a set of **pre-recordings** which carry the music themes, jingles and standard information transmitted by the radio station throughout the day.

The DJ is the voice on air; they introduce music, news, reports and chat items. Depending on the size of the station they may be required to do multi-tasks such as produce, research or write. Radio stations are becoming more **format** conscious. This means that programming decisions, particularly music choice, is no longer the responsibility of the presenter. To avoid the presenter playing their own taste in music and thus confusing the **signature sound** of the station, the programme directors constantly monitor the station's output. It is a little known fact that few radio broadcasters have played their own choice in music since the introduction in the 1980s of the computerized programme management system. This machine produces printed sheets for the presenter to work from. Each sheet represents one hour of programming and signals all programme junctions, features and all the music the presenter must play during the show. All information is supplied – the track title, artist, time of introduction and length of track. It will inform the presenter whether the track has a **hard end** (H) or **fades out** (F). Ad breaks, news and travel bulletins will also be outlined.

Continuity announcers provide the listener with information throughout the day and night. In the event of a technical difficulty or a change in published scheduling, the continuity announcer will alert the listener and provide information. A cool head is once again absolutely essential, as is the ability to operate a control desk. A good continuity announcer is usually measured by how they behave when everything goes wrong, rather than what they do when it is smooth sailing!

Traffic and weather reporters have a vital role to play; travel information is an important service to the listener, especially during rush hours. An authoritative tone is important, as is a sound knowledge of the area to which you are broadcasting: a mispronounced road name can leave your listeners doubting you. This is a great route into a radio station's top shows: many breakfast shows now have a team or 'crew' supporting the main DJ, and the traffic reporter can often play a major role in the crew by acting as a foil for the presenter. Jobs tend to be advertised in the local press and on station notice boards, but there are also independent companies which service many local radio stations with traffic and weather news from a central studio hundreds of miles away. These jobs are often advertised, as the turnover rate is high.

Production

Commercial Producer, Programme Producer, Research, Music Librarian, Traffic Assistant, Phone-in Operator

The Production department controls the station's sound, selecting the music to be played, which needs to be done in accordance with the station's style, sound and key audience. Depending on the style of the station, you may need to be knowledgeable about music or clued-up on current affairs. Programmers are more interested in hands-on experience than anything else, so anything you can do to gain experience, e.g. hospital or college radio, etc., will be invaluable.

Larger stations will have a commercial production department, but smaller stations may have a presenter responsible for this area, or they may contract out the work to another company. Formal qualifications are not required, but the ability to write good radio scripts is essential. There is also a section called 'traffic', which looks after the scheduling of commercials and promotions, and many people find their way into the production side by becoming a traffic assistant. (Traffic in this instance is nothing to do with travel reports – it refers to the traffic of pieces of tape or pre-recorded material.)

Programme producers produce programmes and aim to target the station's output to attract as many listeners as possible. The producer has the ultimate say in what the audience hears. On a **live programme**, the producer will gather together **scripts** beforehand for the presenter to read at given points. With the assistance of an assistant or researcher, the producer will have lined up live guests to be interviewed by the presenter. Before the programme begins, the producer will have drawn up the **running order** – in most live shows this is constantly redrawn to allow for news flashes, or late or non-appearing guests which spoil the producer's plans. Often producers initiate programme ideas, so a creative mind is important. They also have to raise money for programme ideas and organize a budget and ensure it is adhered to, so a financial and business head won't go amiss.

A degree-level education is advisable and experience within the industry, probably as a journalist or researcher on a similar programme or radio station, is needed to become a producer. I would strongly recommend having some solid IT skills and knowledge of the Internet. Producers tend to be people who thrive in a fast-paced environment.

Producers have to be people people: to perform at the microphone with or without a script, conduct interviews and chair discussions, live or pre-recorded; to be responsible for a moving story, amending and updating material as required; to be responsible for thinking through and around editorial problems, developing realistic alternative strategies and approaches; and to offer ideas for items, programmes and series. They have to be team players, leaders and inspirers.

They have to be responsible for studio production of live and pre-recorded programmes, to respond to breaking stories whilst on air and to resolve technical difficulties, to suggest new angles on existing stories, and means of moving the story on, and to put forward stories not yet covered. Flexibility – the ability to adapt and work effectively with a variety of situations, individuals or groups – is a must. The production manager's role involves a lot of responsibility, especially in the areas of money and budgets, which are becoming increasingly important as budgets get tighter and broadcasters become more demanding. They also have responsibility for general administration and the management of staff, both creative and operational. Good financial skills and managerial qualities help here. A clear overview of the **production process** and understanding of the funding of radio are vital. A production manager may go into production but more usually would progress up the managerial path in a larger organization, such as the BBC, or into management in a small production company.

The studio manager is responsible for booking and setting up the studios for each programme. Whilst the show is **on air** the studio manager is responsible for operating the tape recorders, mixing microphones and bringing in pre-recorded sound such as the station's jingle. Editing and technical skills are vital.

Researchers are expected to do a wide variety of tasks such as going through the running order of the programme, checking scripts and querying things, finding good stories and ideas and helping to set up productions. They are most active in areas such as history, science and current affairs. Being thorough, organized and knowing the facts of a story – and also having a bit of flair – all helps to make a good researcher.

The phone-in operator is a vital part of any radio station, as it is their role to provide the first link between the station and the public.

This job involves taking **requests** and **dedications** and working out who can be trusted to speak on air. They need to explain certain procedures to callers, such as that they must switch off their radio at home to avoid howling **feedback** obscuring their voice. Liaising with the producer as to who is calling and on what subject is a vital part of the job. This job has quite a lot of responsibility but is often given to the relatively inexperienced – once they have proved they are trust-worthy!

Sales and Marketing

Sales staff are key to the survival of a commercial radio station. If the sales team cannot obtain sufficient advertising revenue the station will fail no matter how good the programmes are. Sales staff must have an outgoing personality, get on well with clients and, above all, be able to close a deal. There is also an element of routine administrative work.

Larger stations will have full-time promotions and publicity managers; smaller stations may have a presenter whose job it is to oversee these activities. Promotions are activities such as **road shows** or attendance at major local events, and may involve working with sales departments on sponsorship. Publicity work is aimed at achieving press and TV coverage for the station. Formal qualifications are not usually required, but you need good ideas and the ability to plan and see a project through to completion.

Every radio company needs someone to feed out interesting stories about their programmes to the press and to offer pictures of performers and advance copies of programmes for critics to preview. A lot of creative writing also takes place in the production of **listings** – details of the content of programmes, which newspapers and magazines will print in advance so that viewers can decide what they are going to listen to. Listings magazines are extremely popular and also need constant streams of information about programmes.

Talent Management

Agents

Most presenters/performers are recruited and looked after within each production by the programme director, executive producer or producer. For drama productions, casting directors are used, and these specialist individuals usually work as freelancers, supplying their services to a wide number of different productions. They keep large quantities of tapes cataloguing the skills and **cast types** of thousands of individuals.

Agents are employed by presenters, actors, singers, etc., to do deals with radio companies. They therefore generally only represent people that radio stations would want to employ. However, some companies do employ agents in consultancy roles and also use former agents as 'talent managers' to help 'massage' the egos of the main performers and keep them loyal to their station. If you want to work as an agent, you will have to start as a junior at one of the big talent agencies, which are mainly based in London, and look after television, radio and film performers. Most agents develop their own 'client list' and earn their money by taking a commission (15 per cent is a usual fee) from their particular clients' earnings. (See Do I Need an agent?, pages 59–60.)

Writers

Radio Drama, Writing, Scripts and Continuity Material

Radio has a good reputation for helping writers. The BBC pretty much broadcasts all the UK's radio drama programming. It doesn't generally pay well but the BBC gets through nearly 1000 hours of radio drama per year, so there is a demand. The great thing about writing for radio is that script readers rarely reject scripts just because they are written by unknowns. As ever, if you can establish a contact with a script reader then you at least have a good chance of having your work read, although you can also try an agent. Take your **portfolio** along to a writing agent and see what happens. Agents like to have a healthy quantity, quality and variety of clients so they always have something to offer a producer when approached.

Whether it is creative writing, news scripts or documentary narratives, scriptwriting is a vocation, a job in itself, not something you expect to be 'promoted' up from. For news, radio journalists write news copy from information gathered from news services, network feeds, field reports, interviews, recordings, and other sources. In a typical radio operation, most writing is done by producers, reporters and anchors rather than by separate writers.

Where a production needs one, the writer is probably the most important creative link in the whole industry. In drama and comedy, writers hold the power to determine whether the show is a success or not. The scriptwriter needs to be a talented and entertaining writer and, with radio, needs to be able to allow for the listener to have their visualization of the set and characters, etc. On short or one-off series the scriptwriter will invent their characters and see them through to the end. On soaps like Radio 4's *The Archers* the scriptwriter will be one of many and will have to handle new characters invented by other writers.

There are many short courses in script writing available at colleges as well as forming modules of media degrees. The main thing you need is proof that you can write and that you have ideas. If you have experience in journalism, in writing advertising copy or radio programmes, then it is clear that you are interested in writing and have achieved proven success.

The list above is not an exhaustive table of all the jobs available; different stations have different job descriptions. In the BBC, however, the structure is much clearer and many radio jobs have an obvious equivalent in television, so that the cross-over between radio and TV becomes much easier.

CHAPTER 11

Jobs in New Media

There seems to be no clear or established route into new media jobs akin to the traineeships and postgraduate courses that dominate entry into the traditional media of newspapers and broadcasters. Most schools of journalism now offer modules or whole qualifications in **online journalism**. *However, these are yet to produce a sufficient number of graduates to satisfy the considerable demand for people to work in the ever-expanding web business and web-related industries such as* **CD ROM production** *and* **gaming**.

The majority of the top jobs in new media have been taken by experienced existing media professionals like Paul Campbell, the **CEO** of new media company Liberty Bell. These people have transferred their skills, be it from television or print, to new media. But increasingly **web site operators**, design companies and interactive departments of TV companies want to recruit directly from universities or colleges. Similarly, many graduates now want to actually start their careers by going straight into online work.

What is less clear is how they will do that. As in all areas of the media it is necessary to gain qualifications and to possess some skills for the job you wish to land. For the areas available in new media there are simply hundreds of courses available all over the country, in design, graphics, programming and coding, etc.

To work in the new media sector, you do need more than a passing acquaintance with or interest in the Internet. Technologically, I'm no genius. I am certainly not fluent with **HTML**. But I've never been afraid to learn and I've done some weekend courses that have shown me that software can do much of the tricky stuff for me.

However, there are certain factors that give any web wannabe a clear head start. Work experience, as with all media (and indeed most professions), is vital. The benefits of formal training are clear; a good grounding in law, for instance, is as important on the web as it is anywhere else if libel suits are a possibility. But the very nature of the web is so revolutionary that much of what is learnt in one year in a journalism degree may well be outdated by the next. The working practices of the web are also far less established than they are in broadcast or print and so it might also be difficult to know what to teach to a new media student. You can, of course, teach yourself web skills by familiarizing yourself with relevant software packages, e.g., PhotoShop, Homesite, Dreamweaver, or Flash, or you can go on a course.

Web sites need to be built for businesses, online shops, organizations, the self-employed, schools and colleges, and to cover charities and health issues; the list goes on. Company **intranets** need to be designed for training and information. Presentations need to be designed for businesses, training and sales. Kiosk presentations are used in public spaces, art galleries, museums and shops, etc., to inform visitors. DVD interface development for domestic film DVDs, CD ROM presentations, game development and interactive art ... If this is the area of interest for you, you will not be stuck for ideas about which way to take your specialization. Below you will find a list of some of the key jobs available in new media. They range across the board, and need different levels of skills and knowledge of programming and design. It is not a comprehensive list but aims to furnish you with an idea of how this section of the industry works.

There are companies who specialize in liaising with clients and overseeing the design and production of a project, ensuring it follows the clients' specifications. They are equally responsible for ensuring that nothing unfair is asked of the design team; their function is similar to that of an agent – keeping both parties happy. Some of the work will be undertaken in-house, but the more technologically advanced stuff will probably be subcontracted to a specialist company.

There are three categories of new media jobs – design, editorial and technology.

Design

Graphic design companies are responsible for anything from designing web sites and **interactive multimedia** to the traditional graphic design production of print materials. New media design comes under a slightly more refined banner, and such companies tend to only deal with design for the digital age, leaving the print materials to more traditional companies. Here are some of the key jobs involved in the design area of new media.

Trainee Graphic Designer

As a trainee graphic designer you would work with experienced designers and coders to help produce web sites and other new media content such as CD ROMs and **interactive web** or television facilities. A formal qualification in design and an understanding of how design is used in new media formats is mandatory, although years of experience are not. The qualifications you would need to gain an entry-level position in graphic design (such as a BA in design) should have supplied you with knowledge of HTML and an awareness of industry software packages such as PhotoShop and Flash.

Database Designer, Developer

Designing and developing databases involves dealing with huge amounts of data and placing it in a format that can be easily understood and accessed by various members of the team. Database designers and developers can come from pretty much any area of IT. Experience with large quantities of data for analysis and reporting would be of great value. It would generally involve working with programmes similar to Microsoft SQL Server Database. Database administration experience, and knowledge and experience of developing reporting applications using VB, ASP and other tools like Crystal, is normally required.

Game Designer

Game designers often work from the first idea to the finished package of a game. They take the initial idea (often their own) of, say, a racing game; then they think up a story line for the game, perhaps a race based upon the Isle of Man TT. Next come the character designs and the design of the vehicles that players can choose from. Backgrounds and terrains that players can drive through would follow. At this point some game designers turn to programming experts to assist them through the complicated final areas of design programming. In this case the programmer will simply take the game designer's plans and programme the computer to produce them on screen. Some game designers are qualified to see the project through from initial idea to conclusion, which has the benefit of their being able to retain complete control of the game. It also keeps production costs down because fewer people are involved.

Interactive Designer

Interactive designers work specifically with interactive facilities. They work with PhotoShop and similar graphics packages to design and deliver new services across all digital interactive television platforms and the web. Such designers usually have experience in graphic design in relation to the web or interactive TV, but some come across from TV production to digital **interactive TV**. Knowledge of **digital TV platforms** and technical differences are generally required to enable design of new formats, with an understanding of how they can be used. Understanding of production and commissioning processes is necessary, as is the ability to liaise with production teams with an understanding of their pressures and responsibilities. Designers may be required to work on database systems for projects already under construction, although such tasks will usually be delegated to the most junior designer on the team.

3D Animators

The games industry is the most popular place for 3D animators, but plasticine animation – working with basic models and programming them into a computer – is also an important area. 3D development has expanded with speed over the last five years or so. Within the games and movie industries the main jobs are model designers, animators and programmers. A perfect example of this sort of work can be seen in the *Wallace and Gromit* films.

Sound Design

Sound designers literally design the sound for web sites, CD ROMS and games. Rather than create music, sound designers edit tunes to fit a game or section of a site, and supply sound effects to fit the action.

Music Composers

New media composers work in a similar way to mainstream composers but concentrate on writing music for games, CD ROMs and web sites to a specific brief, usually from the web designers. The music may serve as a theme tune to a site or game, and it could be programmed to change as the scenes of the game change or the site pages change.

Web Designers

Technical skills are not paramount but you do need to feel comfortable with programming and codes. Web designers tend to be stronger on graphic design ability and qualifications, with a particular concern for the aesthetic look of a site. They are also needed to design effective and innovative database systems that support new media projects, and to produce design documentation that can be followed by other members of the development team. They also look after the maintenance of web sites after they have gone 'live'.

Editorial

This category includes anyone from writers and journalists to advertisers and education experts. Advertising agencies now nearly always have new media divisions that supply marketing and advertising either in conjunction with a design company, or for the client for whom the designer is working. Magazine and book publishers, particularly with media and technology specialist publications, will produce CD ROMs to accompany materials in the magazine or book itself. These CD ROMs are often accompanied by web sites. Interactive CD ROMs and web sites are vital to a modern publisher's activities.

Project Manager

A project manager has a fairly traditional managerial role and responsibilities – new media projects require close managing of time and resources in the same way as old media projects do. The project manager also co-ordinates the team effort and keeps the team motivated towards the completion of the project at hand. Good verbal and written communication skills are needed for this role and for liaising between the client, who may have ordered a web site with particular specifications, and the design team.

Project Specialist

Project specialists develop and produce documentation to support web design and development projects. They also assist with departmental business management, project tracking, field communications, web production, production quality assurance, etc. Project specialists are experienced communications professionals with editorial and technical writing skills, who participate in and lead the production of complex information and media systems. Experience in producing technical documentation in support of design-driven projects for the Internet or other media is a normal requirement, as well as working with an internal production team. This is a managerial position so project management experience and expertise in project management software are also useful. A degree, as always, is necessary, with a focus in a creative or technology discipline.

Editor

A managerial position not dissimilar to that of a traditional newspaper editor. Controlling style and content according to the brief given by company directors, the editor fills a consultant-style role for web sites. Editors may be required to develop current ideas and systems within the site they edit; they may also be involved in marketing – submitting projects to search engines, developing strategy for marketing to **portals**, and developing strategies for improving placement in search engines. The editor is usually in charge of a team of journalists, programmers, designers and researchers, and has either risen through the ranks of web research or programming, or has come across from old media editing.

Professional Developer

Professional development of web sites and interactive facilities, etc., involves working with designers and programmers. Developers tend to be ex-designers who work, sometimes on a freelance basis, with web designers to maximize the potential of their facility. A sound knowledge of Flash, JavaScript, etc., is mandatory. Developers may also be asked to advise the web company on software programming and training schemes for staff.

Web Promoter

The promoter's main task is to develop and execute online national consumer promotions and all necessary support materials. They work with sales managers and provide sales teams with web-only presentations, web enhancements of standard packages and custom-made proposals. The ability to manage budgets, contracts, timelines and contest fulfilment is necessary. Promoters also manage promotional web-based relationships with the online and on-air advertising sales teams, web production, programming, on-air production, on and off-air creative, legal and the enterprises groups to create opportunities for advertisers. This usually includes brainstorming, developing and executing the promotions, and the writing and execution of packages, as well as the implementation of the various types of promotions (network initiatives, web enhancements and web-only promotions) and custom promotions on the web site. Web promoters are usually individuals who have worked within advertising and new media, as the job combines both fields of expertise.

Interactive Television Senior Producer

A senior producer is in charge of a number of producers and researchers in the editorial development of interactive television and web services. Duties involve taking the lead in delivering these services and keeping the team motivated, as well as being responsible for producing pilots which demonstrate the potential of interactive television and the web, and its evolution into a high-speed, multimedia platform. Understanding of production and commissioning processes is essential. As team leader the senior producer needs an appreciation of the impact and potential of interactive television and the web to its various users.

Web Producers

Producers in the new media sectors work alongside designers and editorial staff to express requirements for content delivery, look, feel and functionality of web sites. They deliver software projects, providing support as required, as well as testing development work and ensuring all work is well documented and accessible. They have the ability to delegate to a team of researchers and assistants, depending on the size of the operation. Producers have to be natural team leaders, able to communicate easily, and with the ability to translate user and client requirements into technical solutions. In some cases they assist with the design of the page and/or interactive facility. It is the producer's responsibility to keep abreast of developments in technology and computing in areas relevant to the project, and so maximize team strengths and deliver the best possible package to the end user and client. Management skills similar to old media producers are also needed. Basic maths is useful for calculating budgets and staff costs, etc. You need to be able to get on with lots of people, as there is often quite a number of interested parties involved, including TV programme and production teams. Web experience, i.e. how to write for the web, an understanding of design, a working knowledge of **HTML**, and an awareness of your target audience and what they want from a site is also required of top producers.

Interactive Television Team Assistant

You need to be a team player with the ability to generate creative ideas, treatments and formats for interactive programming for television and the web. The ability to work collaboratively with technical, design, editorial and project management personnel is required. A team assistant provides administrative support and collates statistical information – keeping records up-to-date and providing administrative support to management, collating information and maintaining office systems. This means solid organizational skills are needed. As for computer or programming skills, knowledge of MS Word, Excel and PowerPoint, or similar programmes, is important.

Interactive Television Research

Interactive researchers deliver new services across all **digital television platforms** and develop enhanced and interactive television services. Most interactive researchers come through TV production or have research experience in a similar field, but in this area knowledge of digital TV platforms and technical differences is also required. Understanding of production and commissioning processes is necessary, and is often gleaned from old-style TV experience.

Web Research

Researchers on the web compile and prepare content for web sites, games, CD ROMs and interactive facilities. Editing skills are necessary, as a large part of the job involves editing audio and video tapes for the web. Researchers ensure that a consistent editorial style is maintained, so they need strong writing skills. Knowledge of **HTML**, editing packages and PhotoShop is necessary for programming the results of any research.

Web researchers also provide support to the editorial team in preparing material for use on interactive platforms. They support new projects and existing output and ensure daily maintenance of the site, informing the editorial team of useful content and market information as they discover it.

The role of researcher will typically cover interviews, original features, quizzes and creating storyline-related content where necessary – say in a web site linked to a TV programme or soap opera. The web researcher will report directly to the producer and will be a key support for the team. Web research can also involve sourcing images and chasing copy for the content team, and seeing through the acquisition of material such as photos, video and audio files. Writing and journalism skills are useful, and there are good possibilities for crossover between standard research and web research.

Network System Administrator

These are responsible for system and network administration and support in the development and production of systems. Such systems may hold company databases or carry a network facility, so related experience in networking, etc., is often required, along with a solid understanding of hardware and network configuration, such as mySQL and Oracle database. Knowledge of programming and related skills often include Unix, DNS, sendmail, Shell and Perl scripting.

Online Editor

Online editors have similar skills to traditional editor types: good research, writing and editing skills, the ability to research, edit and write reviews of web sites, online services, articles and software in English. An understanding of the web and related subjects, programming, etc. is absolutely necessary, but to different standards depending on the company. An awareness of digital technology and how it can be used and built on to assist the quality and availability of the web site is useful.

Editorial Trainee

Editorial trainees need creative minds and great ideas which they can communicate through sound writing ability. Basic editorial skills are also necessary, and most editorial assistants have experience with newspapers or magazine. An awareness of the potential of digital technology is important. As a trainee you would assist in the development and maintenance of the homepage or category sites, or could join an interactive TV project. Any company will require evidence of sound writing skills and editorial judgement, which can be gained through writing courses at colleges or through a degree in English and/ or media studies.

Multimedia Authors

Multimedia authors are experts in applications such as Director and Flash. They work with the designer and web site builder to help navigate the site, provide navigation structure for users of the site and programme interactive facilities between the end user and the interface.

Image Creators and Photographers

These are involved in creating, sourcing and editing the still images required for a project. Photographers take pictures of specific objects, people or configurations as ordered by the web, game or CD ROM designer. Still frames of moving images may also be used, for instance in the character selection section of a game. So, photography skills and basic programming knowledge are needed.

Educational Development Team

These people specialize in CD ROM and online learning: writing, design and production. The material is aimed for educational purposes, such as support packages for GCSE and A-level or High School Diploma, language courses and reference materials such as encyclopedias. Depending on the size of the company, employees may only write the materials, but larger companies would have their own design and production departments.

Technical

You need, obviously, an understanding of the technical side of the web and interactive media. You will have the ability to code in **HTML** and the ability to take on a range of **programming languages** and **software packages**. An understanding of software development would be useful. As a trainee you would find yourself at the centre of new technology developments. The BBC is taking on some trainees in this area and will almost certainly expand its intake in the future.

Programmers and Web Site Builders

Basically programmers write the code to create web sites, games and CD ROMs according to the plan given by a game, web or CD ROM designer. They are experts in such codes as **HTML**, **Flash** and **Java**, which are all used to create sites. They will work in degrees of complexity from simple, perhaps personal or small business sites, to multimedia interactive sites with links, games and complex graphics. If games are included in the site, the programmer would take his or her lead from a game designer.

Web Engineer

Engineers are people that enjoy working with artists and designers in translating visual page layouts into working code. Engineers write clean code and create **template structures** for web site construction whilst ensuring compatibility across browsers and platforms. This is not a purely production job: they also contribute to the design process and participate in decisions that affect the presentation of information. **HTML**, JavaScript and a working knowledge of graphics production tools XML or Flash are typically required of the web engineer.

Web Development Team Assistant

The web development team builds the applications that power sites. Working together with producers and designers, the assistant helps to develop systems that deliver the content. Experience with **HTML** or Perl or similar **programming techniques** is helpful when applying for a job like this. Commercial development experience is also welcomed, even from outside the new media sector. Assistants need to be team players, able to communicate easily, and with enthusiasm for the Internet.

The above jobs are not an exhaustive list because of the number of changes that occur every week in relation to the net and the web. There is no doubt that familiarity with the Internet and its capabilities will stand many people in good stead as the number of jobs in this area increases.

Getting a Job

CHAPTER **12**

Getting Started

Build Your Own History!

The one thing you're going to need when you apply for a job in the broadcasting world is a 'history'. If you've done nothing remotely connected with broadcasting or new media then you're going to have to build your own past – it's a bit like being James Bond – 'We can give you a new identity . . . Mr Bond . . .'. Any prospective employer is going to want to see how you've been gagging to get into the media since before you were born. You should have been writing leader articles for The Times *by the time you reached 10 years old, and running your school dances and discos as soon as you were a teenager. If you didn't actually do this, then you should think more carefully. Talk to your parents and friends; ask them whether you've ever done anything which can illustrate your interests in the media . . . anything. I'm not encouraging you to lie – just to polish the truth up until you can see your face in the shiny bits!*

How to Get In

Take my advice – it's much easier to get into a broadcasting job once you're on the inside. I have always said to broadcasting wannabes tempted to turn their nose up at what they see as a lowly job offer – take it and use it as a springboard. Get into a station as record librarian or newsroom runner and you soon get to hear of other job opportunities on the grapevine. A large number of jobs don't get advertised outside the building, and even when they do, the jobs are often spoken for long before an interview takes place.

Who You Know or What You Know?

Many people find that, in the UK industry, it is *who* you know, not *what* you know. There is a large effort being made to establish a realistic racial and social mix among broadcasting staff within radio and TV stations throughout the UK. Sex discrimination is less of a problem, but there are roles which are male dominated and roles which are female dominated, so some jobs are easier to get because of your sex and some are more difficult – that's life! This is where 'who you know' comes into play: a recommendation about someone by an existing trusted employee is a gift to the employer. If you don't know anyone already in broadcasting, do not fear: **networking** is a valuable skill and it's never to soon to start. If you can get a related job, say in journalism, then you will frequently find yourself socializing and working with a plethora of media types. When you get your first job, be it paid or unpaid, start talking to people and get to know them. Seek out good contacts, get their phone numbers and email addresses and keep in touch. It does make a difference who you know.

Rejection

Be prepared to be knocked back more than once. Some companies will always answer letters as a matter of courtesy, others won't. Remember, those people who make it get rejected as much as the people who don't. The difference between those who make it and the rest of the masses is that they grab every chance they get.

Preparing For Battle

Before you begin your job hunt, ensure that you have the energy to mount and pursue your personal sales campaign, and money for travel, letters and phone bills. The Internet can help you a terrific amount in the early stages – a lot of people can take your application by email these days, and you can send sample tapes, photos and CV details as attachments. But you are going to need a fund of some sort to help make your applications look different from the thousands of other hopefuls.

Apart from pen, paper, etc., I'd suggest you get your hands on *The Blue Book of Broadcasting*, published annually by Taylor Nelson Sofres Tellex (their publications website is www.tellex.press.net). This gives you an invaluable insight into the structure of all the companies you want to write to and who holds which job (managing director, programme producer, etc.) within them. I also recommend that you arm yourself with an up-to-date copy of the *Radio Times*, *TV Times*, or any publication which gives you more details about a programme than just the promo blurb. What you want are the names of the production team and the top person to whom you might write. You can, of course, get that by taking a note from the screen or listening to the credits at the end of each programme, but the **production credits**, as they are known, go so fast or are now so small that they can sometimes be difficult to catch. The production credits are also a good way of seeing how many people are actually employed on a programme, and so how many jobs might be up for grabs! On some shows (especially **sequence programmes**) there might be a different producer each day, but usually there's an editor or an executive producer common to the whole strand.

MIKE'S WISE WORDS – 34

If you believe that you have what it takes to make it in broadcasting, then check out the list below and see if it describes you and your skills.

1. Ability to communicate – written and verbal.
2. Confidence.
3. Ability to work under pressure (the best broadcasters work best under pressure).
4. Stamina.
5. Ability and desire to learn new skills. The broadcasting industry undergoes constant updates in technological equipment.
6. Enthusiasm.
7. Team skills, to be able to work as part of a team. Even when you are at the top, you still have to muck in.

Reasonable education achievements are important and it is advisable to be equipped with a full, clean driving licence. Transferable business and personal skills are also necessary – organizational skills, computer literacy and a good sense of humour will all make your life easier.

Networking

Crucial to success and to building a successful artistic career is networking – this is how the industry works. Employers will work with people they know and trust. Networking is a skill that anyone can develop.

Networking is the act of talking to your friends, colleagues and acquaintances, telling them what you are doing, and seeing if they know anyone who can help you. It's also about getting into formal gatherings, like conferences and industry get-togethers, and approaching people whom you believe can help you. Do this by talking to people through a shared interest. Seek their guidance and knowledge to help each other on a mutual basis.

Use every string you can pull to get yourself noticed by people in positions of power. Use relatives and friends who know someone in the business to help you set up meetings with them so that you can pick their brains about the business. This is a lot more polite than calling someone whom you do not know, or barely know, and asking them to pull strings for you. When you get to meet someone who can help, make sure you observe all the rules of politeness in order to keep in their good books.

If you meet someone, whether it is through a bout of work experience or simply out at a **road show**, and you get chatting, make sure you keep in touch with them. Simple two-paragraph emails every month or so, just letting them know how you are progressing, are brilliant – when you hit them with your **showreel** they know the history behind where it came from. Media people are notorious for giving out business cards, so don't feel bad about asking for one and then using it!

As you go about your networking, you must start a file of industry contacts. This is so you can keep track of who you talked to and what you talked to them about, so you don't make a fool of yourself if you meet them again. The little black contacts book is a vital part of any professional's tools.

This part is pretty self-explanatory but, when you finally get called for an interview, it is up to you to be on time, be delightfully charismatic, and to look like you mean business. Look like your photo, by the way, so they don't say 'who on earth is this?' Finally, be prepared with some interesting, funny stories about your background so you can charm them and be engagingly amusing.

Before you get to actually applying for a job (next chapter!) it's imperative that you build a history for yourself – one which shows that you were interested in this strange business back before you were even born!

A large part of the broadcasting industry is based on 'bullshit', but you have to have something on which to build. It's no good trying to kid someone that you became a vital, indispensable part of the GMTV breakfast team if you haven't even set foot through their door! I'm not here to encourage you to tell an untruth, but neither am I trying to make you hide your light under a bushel. I've already told you that use of industry jargon can go a long way in impressing people at the interview stage. Well – so can using names and places, and everyone expects you to 'polish' the facts in your favour, so don't be shy about it!

The Value of Work Experience

Work experience is the most valuable tool in enabling you to show that you're not talking through your hat. A week spent as part of an actual programme team, even if all you did was make the tea and open the post, can show that you know what you're trying to get into.

The best time for gaining such experience is, obviously, while you're on holiday from your full-time education – school, college or university. Or you can earn some valuable experience points during your gap year. But if you haven't managed it by the time you join the job market, don't worry, you can still use a week off from your job as a supermarket packer or hamburger salesperson to get your foot in the door.

Most work experience placements don't pay any money, although some companies pay things like travel expenses. But the work adds a credential that eventually helps get you a job. Studies have found that a large number of applicants who get entry-level jobs have held what are sometimes known as **internships**, often at the same station. A high proportion of the broadcast journalists I've talked to for this book stressed the value of getting work experience during your academic period. Time after time, they said work experience was one of their most valuable school day and university activities.

THE PROFESSIONAL'S VIEW – ANNE MORRISON

Anne Morrison is one of the most respected professionals in the business. As Controller of the Factual Group within the BBC, she is also one of the most powerful women in the industry, and she started her broadcasting career as a work experience intern during her gap year.

> I was due to go to Cambridge, but had a year to wait, and went banging on various doors in my native Belfast. The BBC took me in and gave me some extremely valuable work experience, and that gave me contacts who gave me further work during my time at university. I believe very strongly in the value of work experience and that we have a real responsibility as an employer to look at people while they are with us, and not to exploit them. It's also important for the people who get to work with us to use

their time properly and not just sit watching. It gives someone a proper chance to assess whether they like the business and will fit in – do they like the atmosphere? Is it the right career?

The BBC has had to centralize requests for work experience since Anne's day, because of the larger number of requests, and interns usually get to spend no more than a month with the Corporation. 'It is unpaid work,' says Anne, 'but we do make sure that people are not out of pocket. It also means that if people apply for a job, we know something about them.'

Anne Morrison went back to BBC Belfast, had summer jobs such as working in the record library and then ended up being taken on in London as one of six BBC General Trainees, out of a shortlist of 6000. She has climbed through radio, TV documentaries, producing *Holiday* and *Rough Justice*, and has ended up in charge of an enormous part of the BBC's output – all from that chance of work experience!

Work experience is valuable because you're working in a real operation, not just a college classroom or lab. Even the best courses usually can do no more than give you a background on the duties involved in working in the real world. The sense of competition and achievement when the programme you are working on goes to air cannot be easily replicated in a classroom.

MIKE'S WISE WORDS – 35

Start looking actively for work experience early on. It may take time, so don't be surprised if several weeks or months and many rejections go by before you get your positive reply. It's very competitive but if you really believe you have what it takes, keep trying. Hanging in there shows that you have one of the qualities of a good broadcast employee – persistence. The demand for work experience is high. The BBC, for instance, now has a complete section dealing with work experience matters, and most other companies have specific people who have to deal with applications. The laws governing work experience people are quite strict now, and some companies will take one person at a time, and then only for a restricted length of time.

How to Get Work Experience

This might be another area where you can use contacts to pull strings. Do you, or your friends, have any relatives working in the business? Has anyone you know had reason to make contact with someone in the broadcasting industry at any time – maybe they've been interviewed for a news programme or they work behind the bar at a place where media types go? Use any possible contact you can find to get a foothold – it will help if you can write to someone with whom you have some existing link. And, of course, the higher up the ladder they are, the better your chances of getting what you want.

Whether it's to someone you know, or directly to the person who handles work experience placements, you need to write a short but convincing letter about how you would benefit from an attachment to their **production unit**. Tell the person what you want eventually to do, when you get a job; tell them that you think the experience you will get with them will give you an enormous advantage in knowing what's required to qualify for a full-time job. Also, let them know how useful you will be, even for a week, as a member of their team.

Make it clear that you know their programme or range of productions (all people who work in broadcasting always think that their programme is the most important), and make sure you tell them something that you admire about what they do.

To be sure you maximize your chances of getting a work experience slot, give them a wide variety of dates when you might be available. Try, if you can, to avoid the peak times – school holidays especially. The summer is probably easier to get in, but remember that many broadcast programmes go 'quiet' during that time, and staff who could help you are often away on their own holidays. Before Christmas is good, when programmes get particularly busy and need extra hands.

MIKE'S WISE WORDS – 36

You have to radiate enthusiasm. Writing to a broadcaster saying 'As part of my A-level in media studies I have to do some work experience ...' makes the whole thing sound like a chore rather than a brilliant opportunity. Rephrase your letter to start, 'As part of my A levels we are encouraged to do a period of work experience and I thought this would be a fantastic chance to ...' Suddenly, you sound keen, enthusiastic and like you are actually interested in what they do! Remember, people who work in television and radio are quite arrogant about their position in society. They need to feel that you would give your right arm to get a peek at what they do!

The Right Place

You'll want to get as much out of your allocated work experience time as possible, so make sure you get slotted in to the right department. Use all your skills and talents – if you speak extra languages or have other abilities like computing, shorthand, artistic abilities, or sports achievements it makes you more valuable, so make sure you let them know. You should use all your persistence to make sure you're going to get the right sort of experience and you're not just being used as cheap labour. Once you find yourself on a promise of work experience, ensure that you know what you're going to be expected to do. If you suspect that you're going to be used as a cheap filing clerk or similar, when you should be out with a film crew or in the studio learning the craft, politely refuse. Your objective is to gain a good picture of the work that you will eventually aspire to – what's the point of ending up in the accounts department for two weeks if you want to be a sports reporter?

The First Day

I have always encouraged people who appear really interested in the business. I think it's important to bring fresh blood and fresh thinking into such a creative world. That is not true of everyone who works in broadcasting; some of them are downright defensive and concerned that anyone coming into the office might be after their job. It means that if you get a work experience opportunity, it's up to you to make the most of it.

If you've only got a short time you need to hit the ground running. You need to be bold and inquisitive, rather than sitting quietly in a corner waiting for someone to come and ask you to do something.

We're not all extroverts, but it helps if you have a good line in **self-introduction**. Spotting opportunities to help is good, but it's not always easy to be part of the office conversation that highlights when those opportunities occur. The best thing is to know in your own mind what you will say to anyone who wants to know why you're there. You should also try to find the person – and there's always one – who *really* runs the office: the person who gets asked to organize the collection for leaving presents, and chivvies the others. Introduce yourself to that person and try to stick with them, so that they talk to you about how the day works and who's doing what. If there are any meetings that staff get called to, make sure you go along too. No matter how overwhelming they might feel, they are great for getting you noticed straight away, and you should always ask someone to make sure you are introduced to everyone at the beginning.

MIKE'S WISE WORDS – 37

A lot of working people feel slightly uneasy and unsure about what to do with work experience people, so they often leave them to their own devices. You sometimes have to seize the initiative and make your own learning opportunities. Spotting someone who is doing something interesting and asking if you can watch is always useful, but be prepared for rejection as well – some people just don't like being watched. And don't lean over someone's shoulder unless they invite you ... they might begin to think you're a management spy! Offering to get teas or coffees is always a good introduction – broadcasting runs on the stuff (although they do say that in the BBC canteen you can't tell the difference between the two!).

Keep a Diary

Make sure you keep a note of everything that you do, so that you can look back on it and reflect on some of the lessons you learned. Something which appeared quite irrelevant at the time might suddenly drop into place for you, long after you've left. Also, don't forget to start that all-important contacts book. Gather as much information from your time there as you possibly can.

The aim of work experience is to gather sufficient knowledge of the broadcasting business to enable you to make the right choices about working in it when you want a full-time job. Don't always go for the obvious parts of the business – they will be under quite heavy pressure from other work experience aspirants. Try finding out about freelancers in the business and ask if you can tag along with them; think about people like make-up designers who drop in and out of all branches of the media world, or prop-buyers who still get to see what's going on, but from a slightly different angle.

Other Valuable Experiences

There are also some associated areas where you can gain valuable insights and contacts – for instance, the Guardian Edinburgh International Television Festival (GEITF). Every year, the great and good of TV gather to discuss the latest developments in the industry. It costs to go there, and even more to find a hotel in Edinburgh, because a lot of other festivals are going on at the same time. But, what about working there? The GEITF needs stewards and usually advertises for around 20 as the TV festival approaches. The stewards are as much a part of the festival as everyone else. They work in the various sessions and around the conference areas, and they hear the top people in the industry talking about the business. The stewards are also the first point of contact for the delegates when they arrive, and have the most direct contact during the conference: very useful in getting to know who's who in your chosen profession.

There are several other festivals and conferences that you can get into as an intern (details later in the book), and they all have work for keen young people. Just remember with most of them it's first-come-first-served. There's also the two-yearly gathering in Cambridge organized by the Royal Television Society, the Radio Festival set up by the Radio Academy, the Oxford Media Conference and many other industry events that will help you gain valuable insights from the sidelines.

Don't forget that there are other stepping stones that can be useful for your CV. If you want to get into TV or radio drama, then think about working in the theatre. If you want to be a radio news reporter, try your hand on a local newspaper. Sports presenting? Some time with your local football club or similar might pay off as well. Think laterally – your CV has got to testify to your interest in the jobs that you will eventually go for. Hospital and student radio can be added to the list of voluntary things you can do that will give you a better view of the broadcasting vista.

So What Do We Know Now?

- *You have to build a history to show how dedicated you have been to getting into broadcasting*
- *Check your personal skills: if you can't work under pressure, learn new skills, work in a team and write well, you've got a problem*
- *Pull every string you can to get to know the right people – network enthusiastically*
- *Use work experience to help build your knowledge of the business and sharpen your CV*
- *Keep a diary, to reflect on the lessons you've learned and those you still have to learn*
- *Join industry organizations and go to industry events*

Chapter **13**

How to Land a Job

Why Should I Give you a Job?

Anyone can say they would like to work in broadcasting. What distinguishes the person who is serious from the rest is the evidence that he or she has done something practical towards achieving their goal. Be doggedly persistent and committed and try to get involved in any media-related activity, such as hospital or community radio, behind the scenes at fringe theatres, writing for a local newspaper, or your school/college magazine. Other interests which are relevant include photography, sound recording, knowledge of new media graphics, programming, editing skills . . . the list goes on. I have said it before and I'll say it again: you must watch and listen to television and radio and surf the web, especially if you want to be involved in programme making. Producers want to see practical evidence to support your enthusiasm, as well as aptitude and, possibly, some professional experience.

What Have You Got to Offer?

So what can you offer the industry? How can you sell yourself? We are in increasingly cost-conscious times and many employers look for **multi-skilled** people – those who can make a contribution from day one, not clueless youngsters who think broadcasting looks like a bit of fun but have done nothing to get themselves up-to-date with the industry.

Broadcasters are looking for people who know their audience, who can recognize a good story or idea and turn it into good programme material. Although you may be attracted by a particular area of TV or radio, the programme makers of tomorrow will need to work across different media and understand how to package ideas for different markets.

You must have imagination and ideas as well as an instinct for a good story. Communications skills, writing and IT skills are all a must and a must-mention. There are some common routes in this business, but most people's success stories show that they have carved their own career according to their interests and skills. Broadcast programmes also have to go out on time! Punctuality, efficiency, personality and clarity of communication are essential qualities.

Think about your best skills and assets. How can you express them in the most clear and concise way? When you are preparing for an interview think of the sort of thing you can do and would like to do and support it with your skills: I'd like to be a TV researcher. I am organized and efficient, I can access information from a variety of sources and I am great at communicating – on the phone, by letter and in person.

When applying for jobs it may seem like a good idea to draw attention to yourself, to make your witty and zany personality shine through a humdrum application process. Be careful though: you don't want to embarrass prospective employers. Some people send audio-cassettes in breakfast cereal packets for early morning shows. That sort of thing is okay as long as you have an original, inoffensive idea to get yourself noticed. (Obviously there is no point in sending cereal packets now because it's been done too many times.)

MIKE'S WISE WORDS – 38

There are lots of tricks to try to get your application noticed. But try not to go over the top when drawing attention to yourself. I remember when Bob Geldof and his band launched a new single and in an effort to score as much radio play time as possible they sent a reminder of who they were in the post to every radio station in the UK. They were the Boomtown Rats: they sent a dead rat in the post to every top DJ! They did not get much **air play**.

I've also come across all sorts of tricks to get me to notice people's applications. Some people, usually girls, add a few stardust sprinkles and a chocolate bar to eat while I 'take a break' to study their CV. Others have attached a yellow sticky with a note on saying 'Must see this person' – as if I have already read it and written a note to my secretary – but one of the cleverest ones was from a girl (why is it the girls do all the best tricks?) who enclosed two postcards with her application. One was all

dark and gloomy and addressed back to her with the words 'No –
now go away' on it; the other was much brighter and said, 'Yes,
please, I like your style, come and see me straight away'. The
'Yes, please' one also had a stamp on it … guess which one got
posted?

Volunteering

Probably the easiest way to get your first break is to volunteer your
services: be willing to do whatever needs doing. There are dozens of
simple jobs on a radio station that need doing and doing well, but
often the production staff are too busy doing other things. This is
where volunteers can make their mark. Taking phone calls in the
studio and helping out on events like road shows will get you 'brownie
points' and show that you are keen. It will also get you noticed by the
people who matter. If you are approaching your local radio or TV
station, ask if they need help in the record library or with phone-ins; it
will show you how programmes are put together and make you part of
a team. If you are approaching a local newspaper, ask if they need help
in their **cuttings** library or with any administration duty: be prepared
to start off making tea or doing the sandwich run.

Once you've got your foot in the door, try to work in as many
different departments as possible. Although your main aim may be to
become a presenter, web site designer or top-level producer, it is vital
that you know how hard everyone else works behind the scenes, and
it will let you appreciate their responsibilities as well.

If volunteering is a financial impossibility, there are other ways.
Check out Chapter 9, Jobs in TV, Chapter 10, Jobs in Radio, or
Chapter 11, Jobs in New Media for some of the basic positions, which
can usually be got hold of without a lot of experience.

Read the *Guardian* and its web site MediaGuardian.com, the
Radio Magazine and *Broadcast* wherever possible, sign up for the
ukradio.com and radioacademy.org email alerts, and attend Royal
Television Society and Radio Academy events when they are in your
area. You really need to keep in touch with the business: who's who,
who and what is popular in radio and TV, what new technological
advances have been made, etc. The above publications should help
you learn about these things.

There is no argument for not getting experience in radio or TV. No
matter how good you think you are, until you've got some research
experience or **flying hours** on your CV, no one is going to take you on.
Find a hospital, student or community radio station, and start with an
enthusiastic and open mind. Better still, get experience at several

stations, demonstrating you are versatile and aware that there are several different ways of running a station.

Getting to the Top

Those people who reach the highest level of management in media organizations do so as a result of hard work and extensive careers that span their chosen areas and a range of other areas as well. They have worked across disciplines within their sector. They understand how the industry works. They have confidence that they can work effectively. They will have attended and succeeded at a number of formal training courses. So, once you've landed a job, don't think the hard work stops there!

Show Willing

If you're being interviewed for an entry-level job, make it clear you're happy to do entry-level tasks – because that's what you will be doing after all. As I've previously mentioned, most beginners in TV start out printing out script pages, scanning the news wires, answering phones and sorting out paper jams in photocopiers. These jobs aren't exactly difficult, but they are important – if not vital – for the smooth running of the studio. One unanswered phone call or misplaced script page can wreck a programme. Show them that you know that and will never let it happen. Be trustworthy.

Applications

When preparing to write applications it is essential that you do some background research to ensure that you know all about the company and that what you have to offer is suitable for that company. Do not approach an independent production company that specializes in dramas with a great enthusiasm for working on quiz shows!

To get to know more about the independent production companies, get your hands on a copy of the *PACT Directory of Independent Producers*. PACT stands for Producers Alliance for Cinema and Television and the directory lists all PACT member companies. This way you can rest assured that the companies you are applying to are decent, well-run organizations. Details can be found in Chapter 14.

Both your CV and covering letter must be word-processed. Always post applications first class or hand deliver them. Your envelope may go unopened if you make your application second class. There may be thousands of applications for one position: don't give them an excuse to save themselves the work of reading yours.

MIKE'S WISE WORDS – 39

Here are some helpful hints to ensure that you approach television and radio stations well prepared and with the right sort of attitude.

Always make yourself as attractive as possible to your prospective employer. List such things as:

Word processing skills	Spreadsheet production	Language skills
Team membership	Practical problem solving	Marketing skills
Ability to work under pressure	Reliability	Tenacity
Common sense	Communication skills	Problem solving
Stamina	Working relationships	Fitness

About Your CV

A CV is a marketing document. Unlike other industries which employ personnel staff to filter job applications, your CV may arrive directly on the desk of the person with the authority to give you a job. This person will be very busy. Your CV has only seconds to make an impression.

General CV Tips

Don't be afraid to give your ultimate career goal in your CV. It shows that you do have goals and that you do think about your future. You can then tailor your skills towards that goal.

It's never a bad idea to include some hobbies. Make sure they are not solitary pursuits, like bird watching, but team ones, like playing in an orchestra. Team sports like soccer or one-on-one activities, such as squash or debating, are usually safe bets. It's important to a prospective employer that you can work either in a team or as an individual, but always amongst others.

Write your CV with the potential employer in mind. Use only the most relevant information about your career, education and skills. Provide an accurate portrait of yourself. Sometimes overselling yourself can be as bad as underselling. You want to be keen and confident but not blasé.

One standard CV for all employers is not enough. Ideally you should tailor your CV to each individual employer, or at least tailor it to the *type* of employer you approach (e.g. broadcaster, corporate sector, education sector).

Writing Your CV

Put your name and address at the top, along with phone numbers and email address. Driving licence, non-smoker (you are, aren't you!) and age should follow. It is usually best to begin with employment (unless you are still studying and want a summer job but your job experience is negligible – in this case put down your qualifications, including what you are studying for at the moment). Employment details should start with the most recent job first – date, place of work, job title. Then subtitle experience, which should include anything you've done that is relevant to the position you are applying for, anything that shows your personal qualities – team sports mean you are team player, head of neighbourhood watch means community spirit and a leader. Next subtitle qualifications, and detail those in the same way – date, where studied, what studied and what result or level gained.

Example CV: Jon Brotherdale

91 Any Street
Oxford
OX2 6LN

jonbr60@hotmail.com   Phone: 01865 559006   Mobile: 07836 637086
DoB: 03/05/1979   Clean Driving Licence   Non-Smoker

Employment
Current	Oxford Blue FM Consultant & Researcher, for radio licence application
2002	March–April: The Sunday Telegraph, Trainee Diarist on diary column
2001/2	October–March: The BBC Format Factory, Ents Dept
2001	April–Sept: Excellent Entertainment Ltd., Press Officer
2000	August: Edinburgh International Television Festival, Steward
1997	Gap Year – Work as Sports Coach, Melmont School, London.

Casual Employment
1999–00	ASA Swimming Teacher (Evenings)
1997–00	Sports Camp Counsellor, Arizona camp, USA (Summer Camp)
1998–00	Lifeguard (Weekends)

Work Experience
2000	BBC Watchdog, Researcher (1 Month)

2000	Carlton ITV, News Researcher (1 Month)
1999	The Cherwell Newspaper, Contributor and Photographer (Oxford Univ.)
1999	Mill End Press, Free Newspaper Dept., Runner.
1997/8	Melmont School Magazine Editorial team (Gap Year School work)
1996/7	The Oldenham Chronicle, Editor (School)
1997	The Oldenhamian Magazine, Assistant Editor (School)
1994	St Henry's School Magazine, Editorial team (School)

Education

1998/2001	Westminster College, Oxford BTh (Hons) Oxon, 2nd Class
1997	A-Levels: Oldenham School, Herts. English Literature (A) Religious Studies (A) Media Studies (B)
1995	GCSEs: St Henry's School, Northwood. 9 passes grades B and above

Achievements and Skills

1998	The London Marathon
2000	Performed in Edinburgh Festival: Comedy Sketches (Barry Cryer, Julian Clary)

Various plays (Am Dram, University and college productions, panto)
Computer literate Word, Lexus, Web skills

Referees

Dr Giles Gill	Ms Lilli Chester
Work Experience Co-ordinator	Managing Director
Watchdog	'Oxford Blue FM'
BBC TV, White City	PO Box 299
London W12 7QT	Oxford OX2 6LN

CV Check List

Remember, the basic aim of the CV is to make the interviewer want to meet you. Don't forget you are selling yourself: you must present and market yourself professionally. The following check list should help you make the most of your expertise and experience:

1. Print your CV on good quality paper, no smaller than 12–point font size.
2. Lay it out carefully with the most relevant key skills and achievements near the top.

3. Centre your name at the top.
4. Don't go into massive detail about your smaller achievements: '9 GCSEs' will do.
5. Have someone read through it when you've finished, checking spelling and points you've missed out!
6. Include anyone who you have worked for that your prospective employer knows and trusts.
7. Give the names of two referees – people who know you well and that *you know* will speak well of you. Make sure you ask their agreement to name them. Some people might be unwilling to give references for personal reasons.
8. Give details where you can be contacted easily – at work, home and your mobile number.
9. You can play about with the order, making sure that you highlight skills and abilities wherever possible. Make the CV work for you and make the most of your experiences.
10. Think about what you have to offer and what you need to learn.
11. Avoid long sentences: bullet points are usually enough. If they want to find out more then they can invite you to an interview . . . tempt your reader, tease them.
12. Use the active tense rather than the passive, e.g. 'undertook various roles' rather than 'various roles were undertaken'.
13. Do not mix fonts. Use bold, italics and underlining carefully. Use black ink and white paper for the CV. Your covering letter can be more flamboyant if you wish.
14. Be concise – keep it to one side of A4. You don't need to inform people at length of a week's work experience with the RSPCA or your Saturday job at a newsagent. Avoid narrative and use key words, keep it short and it will have more impact. Use your space wisely . . . plan it.

MIKE'S WISE WORDS – 40

Make sure you attach a photo of yourself to your application. I know from bitter experience as an interviewer that by the time you get to the end of a gruelling day of interviews, it can be very difficult to remember a candidate who came through the door at 9 a.m. Even if the job doesn't involve appearing on camera or in front of the mike, a photograph can be an invaluable aid in helping to root you in the minds of your interrogators at an interview! Attach your photo back-to-back with an A4 CV with staples neatly in each corner.

Cover Letters

Along with your CV you need a strong, well-written letter. The covering letter introduces you and should complement your CV. It shows you've taken the time to find out whom to contact. It may also give you the edge over someone who has similar skills on their CV, but hasn't bothered to write a covering letter to accompany it. The letter, as with the envelope, must be addressed to the right person with their name and titled spelled correctly. If you don't write to the right person your letter will end up in the bin. 'To Whom it may Concern' letters are included in that. You can call the company and ask for names and spellings, etc. In my experience people tend to be very helpful and sympathetic.

You may also want to include other items, including a **showreel**, photograph and copies of newspaper cuttings.

Don't Beat About the Bush

Get straight to the point. Why are you writing to this particular company and this particular person? What do you want from them: experience? A job? Advice as a newcomer? Let them know immediately: they don't want to wade through hyperbole to get to the point. The letter should sell your CV and your CV should clinch the deal for you. Write to a named person with a job title and specific address.

Be an Individual

This is an opportunity to personalize the communication and speak directly to the employer. It's worth spending time getting it right. As with your CV, your letter should not exceed one page of A4 paper. I would recommend including your email address and mobile phone number as well as your postal address on your letter – this makes you seem easily available and allows the recipient to contact you in whatever way suits them. Give your reasons for wanting to work in any particular area and outline your most recent and relevant experience. It is also a good idea to ask the person to whom you are writing for any advice they can give you. Try to get them to agree to meet you, as it will help you stick in their mind for the future, especially if they can put a face to a name. 'I'd welcome the chance to meet you ...' shows enthusiasm but is not too pushy. And do follow up. Strike a balance between genuine interest and causing irritation.

Your letter can reinforce key points from your CV, but it shouldn't repeat information from it. You might want to mention your selling points, or how your CV meets this need. Flag up relevant points that are expanded on in your CV.

Sending a letter off with spelling mistakes and grammatical errors is akin to saying 'your company and this letter mean so little to me that I couldn't be bothered to spell check it'.

No Apologies Please

Be positive: never send anything that is not your best work. If you feel the need to apologise about your CV layout, the ink splodge on your letter or the crackling sound on your demo tape, tear them up and start again. 'Sorry about my showreel, it was recorded over my old Take That tape and the machine doesn't work very well and I had a cold' – you don't get a salesperson turning up at your door selling you goods by pointing out all the faults with them. Your showreel should be the best you can produce, so there shouldn't be any need for excuses.

Standard letters get standard replies. You have got to make yourself stand out from the crowd, otherwise all you will be receiving back is 'no positions are currently available but we'll put your letter on file'. Always say something positive about your showreel and the station you are sending the letter to, and you should receive a letter that isn't just standard in reply.

Buzz Words

To use in your CV, cover letter and even the interview, these words should hit a keynote with the reader or interviewer. Obviously pick the ones that describe you best and use them sparingly and thoughtfully: no reeling off massive lists of buzz words please!

Analysed, Edited, Motivated, Researched, Approved, Established, Organized, Saved, Award-winning, Experience, Highly Regarded, Initiated, Planned, Sold, Career, Created, Innovated, Prepared, Trained, Completed, Led, Presented, Transformed, Developed, Managed, Reorganized, Leadership, Promotion, Prestigious – these are all buzz words you can use.

MIKE'S WISE WORDS – 41

How selective should you be in applying? Advice varies. You may be recommended to take the scattergun approach and apply everywhere, just in case. But I would advise limiting yourself to stations that are realistic prospects. Make a concentrated effort with those stations. Do your homework. Learn the programme director's name. Learn the station's programme format, coverage area and news philosophy. You can then tailor your application to that station. If there's one where you'd particularly like to work, visit it if possible.

If you really want to succeed in TV and radio you will have to accept that frequent moves from city to city are necessary for professional advancement. In my first years in broadcasting I moved seven times before ending up in London. As disruptive as it may be, it really does help to show how keen and willing you are, and introduces opportunities you may not have come across if you had insisted that London is the only place to work!

Keepsafe

Finally, make sure you keep a careful file of all correspondence sent and received. This will help you in two ways: first, you will be able to see what sort of letter people respond to best. A formal CV with a personal letter addressed to the relevant individual sent by post may receive something like a 80 per cent reply rate, whereas a three-line email with CV as an attachment may only receive a 19 per cent reply rate. Second, a file will help you to keep track of replies which stated nothing would be available for three months – you can then remind yourself to chase them up in three months' time.

The Job Interview

Okay – so your CV and your powers of persuasion have netted you an interview. In a sense, you're back to square one and in the starting blocks again. You need to prepare as much for the interview as you did in trying to get seen.

Make sure you know who you are going to see, exactly what job you are being interviewed for and brief yourself on what the company does. Research, watch and listen to as much as you can.

Dress to Impress

Television and radio are filled with people who are trained to make quick decisions based on how things look and sound; they can't help themselves when it comes to you. Like it or not, you need to look as good as you can. Ladies, dress for success. A smart trouser suit should do the trick. Guys should also go for a neat look, preferably a jacket, dark and understated.

First impressions count. If you walk into your interview in your favourite old jeans and a wrinkled shirt, you've already lost the job. But if you walk in looking like a million dollars, it'll send a message to the interviewer that you're professional. Depending on what type of job you are going for, there are different dress codes that apply. No matter what the job is, though, when you look in the mirror, two words need to come to mind: 'neat' and 'clean'. Some TV jobs require a funky look, and it's important that your interviewers can envisage you working as part of their team. It's a tricky situation – you don't want to look too severe and business-like if you want to be a researcher on a daytime show, and you don't want to look cool and casual if you are looking for a job on a national newspaper. There are, however, two general routes that you could follow when dressing for a job interview, depending on the position.

For a researcher on *Newsnight* or a TV reporter your only good choice is a black or navy blue suit (a skirt version for the ladies is sometimes a good idea, but not necessarily). Even going out on a limb with a light suit is a bad idea. News editors want to know you are going to respect them, and they want you to fit in and be a reliable and trustworthy member of their team. So you want to look like you already work for them. It sounds weird but you can help your interviewer relax as well, and if they enjoy the interview all the better for you.

For a more creative job – pop music researcher, presenter for a children's show, etc. – you have a little more leeway. While you still want to look well kept, you can feel more comfortable. You can forego traditional black/brown/navy for some brighter colours. Ladies should go for smart trousers or a skirt with a smart, newish looking top, be it a fitted tee-shirt or funky shirt. As for the gentlemen, you *can* forget the tie, but nice trousers and a collared shirt are still your best bet for impressing the big bad interviewer.

MIKE'S WISE WORDS – 42

I often think it is a good idea to take breath mints for before – not during – the interview and not chewing gum ... horrible things can happen with chewing gum because you cannot conceive of going into the interview chomping away like a masticating cow. What happens when you arrive in the waiting room still chewing? Oops, I forgot! And yup, you guessed it, there's no bin – so just as you are sticking it under the chair, your interviewer calls you in and catches you at it. Hmmm, not good to display your lack of care of the company's furniture ... So breath mints it is. And finally a pad of paper and a couple of secure, non-leaking pens.

Your Interview Check List

Be Organized

Leave more than plenty of time to get everything organized and to get where you are going. It is amazing how much better things will go if you don't feel rushed or frazzled when you walk in the office door.

Show Off

Try to bring examples of relevant work with you. Ensure you have a suitable carrier – a portfolio for any photographs or written work. If you don't have one then someone you know will. If you don't feel a portfolio is right for you because you have sent work ahead of the interview, at least have an A4 flat folder in which you can stash a couple of extra copies of your CV and copies of your references (even if they haven't asked for any yet, always be prepared).

Hands

Give a firm handshake. No sweaty palms (if you're concerned then run your hands under the cold water tap in the loo just before you go in), practise a decent grip and take note of the size of hand that is being offered to you: if your interviewer is a waif, you don't want to crush her arm with an over-manly shake, and if he is a giant make note to really grip! This shows confidence and grace under pressure.

Eyes

Make eye contact. Looking your interviewer straight in the eye shows that you are confident and honest. This will impress them and make you appear capable. Continue making eye contact throughout the entire interview.

Teeth

Smile at the beginning. Shining your pearly whites show you are easygoing and relaxed. Smiles scream team player. And there is nothing interviewers want more than team players. Obviously don't sit there with a vacant smile through the interview: just act like you're thrilled to be there and you honestly like your interviewer.

Be Gracious

If they offer you a drink, take one. It is easy in an interview to just say 'no thanks' almost as a reflex action. Try not to do this, it is always a good thing to accept someone's offer of hospitality and it will help you avoid getting a dry mouth. I would recommend asking for water – it's cold, so you don't have to worry about spilling it and burning your interviewer, it won't stain if you do spill it, and you don't have to launch into milk and sugar requirements. Also, if you ask for tea or coffee, they'll probably bring it in a cup and saucer. Have you ever heard someone who's a bit nervous trying to put a cup down on a saucer? Castinets, anyone? With a disposable plastic cup you can take sips while you think about your answers ... it will buy you time and give you something else to think about. Sit up straight. Your head-teacher was right – it looks nice and keeps you alert.

Use Your Voice

Speak up, but never interrupt. Be enthusiastic, and try not to answer with just a yes or no – there's nothing worse than an interviewee who doesn't speak unless asked direct questions. Remember that you're selling yourself, so it's important to appear enthusiastic. The key is to elaborate without being an ultra-chatty motor mouth. If you interrupt your interviewer in mid-sentence, you may miss the point. Even if you think you have something ingenious to contribute, wait until they finish.

Suck up

Make comments about how nice the neighbourhood, office, and area is. Try to make some compliments about the surroundings. Say: 'I got here early and I was walking around, I really love ...' This shows off your observational and interpersonal skills (not to mention your punctuality).

MIKE'S WISE WORDS – 43

The best thing you can do for your interviewers is to make their job easier. If interviewers walk out after talking to you feeling like they carried the weight of the conversation and had to do all the work, that is a point against you. Remember they may be interviewing dozens of people, they may be getting bored or the person on the other side of the table might be as unused to interviewing as you are! Take control of the situation and always remain enthusiastic. If your exchange leaves them thinking, 'Hey, I enjoyed that,' that could move you that much closer to hearing that you've got the job.

The Obvious Questions

In any broadcast interview you can expect a couple of definite questions to come up. You will often be asked to name your good and bad points. This is a tricky one. You need to be able to recognize where perhaps you need improvement, but you don't want to give them a reason not to give you the job. The best thing to do in this situation is to avoid any character flaws and go for something that would be classed as just less than ideal ... it need not be true. Something along the lines of 'I have difficulty in saying no to people so

I occasionally end up taking on more then my share of the work'. That sets you up as a team player and a hard worker ... not really a bad point then!

Always try to sell yourself as a problem-solver. Think about the work you have done, the job you had in college, volunteer work you did, or the club that you founded. Then proceed to illustrate how you solved a particular problem by breaking that experience into three parts: the problem you encountered, how you analysed it and, finally, the solution you implemented.

The Horrible Questions You will be Asked (So be Prepared!)

- What interests you most about this position?
- Where do you see yourself in 5, 10, 20 years?
- What is your ultimate career goal?
- Tell me about a project that had a tough problem that you solved.
- What did you like about your last job – (and) so, why did you leave it?
- What separates you from other candidates?

If you prepare careful answers to these questions in advance, you'll be ahead of the game. In each of your answers, try to convey your enthusiasm and ability to be a team player. Remember not to leap in quickly, give yourself time to think and try not to ramble; long answers make it seem like you are struggling to find something intelligent to say.

Any Questions?

Towards the end of the session, the interviewer is going to ask you for any questions you might have. You absolutely must have two or three (no more, this is not a freebie career counselling session) insightful and intelligent questions. Look as if you are thinking about whether you have any questions and then ask an appropriate one from the list you've thought about beforehand. Here's a couple of potential questions:

- How would you describe a typical workday?
- What is the best part of working for this production company for you?

I would not recommend talking money unless they ask you. Money is not relevant at this stage; when you are offered the job you can negotiate, or decline the job if they are not offering enough.

MIKE'S WISE WORDS – 44

Your exit from an interview is almost as important as your entrance. No matter how drained or confused you might be, always try to leave the interview on a positive note. As you shake their hand repeat how interested you are in the job. You may think the interview is over when you walk out the door. It's not. It's not over until someone gets the job – as you leave they will talk about you and you will continue to come up in the following days as decisions are made, so the manner of your leaving is important too!

The Interview Follow Up

If you haven't heard anything after a week, call them, unless they have specified that it will take them a certain amount of time, in which case wait until a day or so after their self-given deadline. No one wants to be a nuisance, but a little perseverance never hurt anyone either. The call will serve to remind the company about the incredible interviewee they don't want to let go. It's not being pushy; it's being persistent. Pushiness is bad, but persistence is good.

There are a few things you can do to follow up the interview to remind people who you are and why you are so truly fabulous. The very day of the interview – not the next day or the day after that – send out a thank you note to your interviewer. Keep it simple, thank them for their time and express how much you enjoyed the interview. If you can, remind them who you are with a comment such as, thank you for your explanation of the BBC's plans for interactivity on their children's programming. This just reminds them subtly of how enthusiastic you were, etc. Make sure to have it in the post ASAP so it is sitting on your interviewer's desk when he or she sits down to make a decision. Also, remember to send a note to everyone who gave you a formal interview, not just to one person. A group of people that want you can hold the key.

MIKE'S WISE WORDS – 45

The more interviews you have, the better you will become at them: practice makes perfect. Ask someone to give you a mock interview before the real thing. Don't lose faith, interviews are not easy but you will crack it!

Programme Idea

Television is a creative medium. If you are going to do well in the media you need to have ideas: programme ideas, ideas about how things should work. When applying for pretty much any broadcasting job you will need to show that you have creativity and reasonable, implementable ideas. This will often be asked of you in the form of a programming format suggestion. I have included one below so that you get an idea of what is expected of you.

'Dare You'
The BBC's Interactive Reality Game Show

Presenter/ Co-cordinator/ Narrator (Suggestions)
Jayne Middlemiss or Zoe Ball

IDEA
Before the first show a display of statistics of each team will be explained to the viewers. Strength, speed, agility, IQ and memory powers, etc., will all be available (think Top Trumps). The viewers may then place 'bets' (no money involved) on each team via the Internet as to who will win that week's task using their interactive facility. The statistics will be updated on the BBC's web site each week according to what happened during the last show. Prizes will be awarded to the viewer selected from those who most accurately 'bet' on the winning team. Top prizes could include the chance to take part in the next series.

DETAILS
Eight contestants are set a task each week, live on air. Each team will be followed by a camera crew, narration will be added in post production by one of the presenters. The contestants may not refuse a task – they have to give it a shot. Obviously they will have to be carefully selected after the tasks have been decided on so that all contestants hold a driving licence if necessary or have no hysterical fear of heights, etc. The tasks must be feasible to complete but also possible to fail so funny situations arise. On many of the tasks a professional will have to be heralded: a professional rally driver or sky diver for example, who is qualified to teach and alert the contestants to safety issues, etc.

COMPOSITION OF PROGRAMME
Recap of last show by key presenter and introduction of professional involved in this week's task.

A short demonstrative talk by the professional involved with the last week's task, helped by the key presenter and aimed at the contestants in the studio.

Highlights of the task set, with narration by second presenter, showing embarrassing failures, etc. (Live face of contestants watching themselves, **iris wiped** into the corner of the shot à la Blind Date.)

Chat with both presenters and teams

Updating team points to the team who won.

The next task will be set at the end of the show. Viewers will have until midnight the night before the next show to place their bets.

EXAMPLES

'Learn to rally drive and race each other'. Each team will be assigned an instructor who will spend a week teaching the team mates to drive rally style. The teams will then face each other for a race, with the winning team scooping the points.

Adapt – Be Flexible

All the advice I have given in this chapter has to be subject to alteration according to the circumstances of the job for which you are applying and the company you are applying to. The BBC, for instance, has forms which you must fill in and makes you tick all sorts of boxes to see whether you conform to certain racial or physical stereotypes – you can get the feeling that all your individuality is being ironed out. Just treat this sort of application as an even greater challenge to make yourself shine through.

Larger companies need more information from you to make sure their workforce is kept in proper balance; smaller ones will be more informal. Stay flexible and treat each opportunity for an application or interview on its own merits. Always ask for advice.

So What Do We Know Now?

- *Think about what you have to offer a prospective employer – your best skills and assets*
- *Be prepared to volunteer for work if there's no other way in*
- *Think how to make your application stand out from the crowd*
- *Make sure all your CV details are relevant to the job for which you are applying*
- *Make sure your cover letter is your best work – wrong names and bad spelling all help to 'turn off' a prospective employer*
- *In an interview situation dress to impress, be confident, prepare*
- *Follow up your interview politely with thank you letters; be patient for the results*

Contacts and Information

CHAPTER **14**

Useful Contacts and Organizations

Getting that first job in this industry can be the most difficult part of anyone's career. It doesn't necessarily get any easier from then on, but at least you'll have some experience behind you and, hopefully, a few contacts that may be able to help. It is a very competitive industry and you need the right qualifications, you need to be really keen, and you need that experience. Every skill, piece of knowledge, training and personal attribute needs to be used and demonstrated to make you more employable than the next person.

The resources in this section will give you a helping hand. There's background information on the different sectors of the industry and descriptions of what the various jobs are. Lists of industry publications will help you do your research and build up your knowledge, along with areas of skill shortages, so you know where there may be employment opportunities. These resources are just a starting point, but will help you be prepared so that when you do get that first break, you can grab it with both hands.

Although they may have been mentioned elsewhere in the book, I want to provide you with a detailed listing of a large number of the organizations that look after this fascinating business of ours. There is also a list of useful contacts where you can find out about Internet radio, competitions you can enter to win the chance to have your own work published or be trained to present on TV. There are also presenting courses, web sites and names and addresses for the UK's top radio and TV stations as well as contact details for new media companies.

America

National Association of Television Production Executives
www.natpe.org
NATPE is 'an alliance of media content professionals'. Membership is available to pretty much everyone who is involved in their area of work. Their web site has a great career centre and loads of up-to-date information on interactive TV.

The Film and Television Action Committee
www.ftacusa.org
An organization set up to ensure fair play for American TV and film workers.

The National Association of Broadcasters
www.nab.org
An association for anyone working in free, over-the-air radio and television. They host shows and conferences and have ideas for radio shows and stations and library resources on their web site.

American Communication Association
www.americancomm.org
For media scholars and practitioners in North, Central and South America and the Caribbean. On their wib site they have essays on the media, TV and radio and links to TV and radio web sites.

Film and TV Connection
www.film-connection.com
An American training ground for on-the-job experience in film and TV studies. They teach digital technology and place students for work experience.

American Federation of TV and Radio Artists
www.aftra.org
Up-to-date broadcast news, new technology information and news, and some sound advice on agents is also available on their web site.

The Hollywood Reporter
www.hollywoodreporter.com
There is a list of all producers and production companies, etc. similar

to the British *Blue Book*. You can order a copy online and find out more about it from the web site.

Some Top US TV Station Web Sites
ABC
www.abcnews.com
Loads of internships, including new media.

Fox
www.fox.com

E! Entertainment
www.eonline.com

NBC
www.nbc.com/

CBS
www.cbs.com

UK Governing Bodies

OFCOM – The Office of Communications
At the heart of the UK's broadcasting and telecommunications industry in the future will be the Office of Telecommunications, a new body set up by the UK government in 2002.

OFCOM has been designed to reflect the changing nature of tele-communications. Modern communication networks mean that telephone calls, fax messages, email, radio signals, TV pictures and online information services are all capable of using digital signals. All these changes in technology are resulting in the restructuring of companies.

OFCOM is set to swallow up the Radio Authority, the ITC, OFTEL, the Broadcasting Standards Commission and the Radio Communications Agency. The 'shadow' organization will be working throughout 2003 and will probably be fully active by the beginning of 2004.

Its web site is www.ofcom.org.uk and all five organizations involved in OFCOM can be reached through the OFCOM website.

At the time of writing OFCOM was in the process of moving to permanent headquarters.

OFCOM
Riverside House
Southwark
London SE1
www.ofcom.org.uk

These bodies are still operational until fully absorbed by OFCOM:

The Independent Television Commission
33 Foley Street
London W1W 7TL
020 7255 3000
www.itc.org.uk

Licenses and regulates commercial television in the UK, investigates complaints from the public and monitors television output. They do not deal with the BBC or S4C in Wales.

The Radio Authority
Holbrook house
14 Great Queen Street
Holborn
London WC2B 5DG
020 7430 2724
www.radioauthority.org.uk

Acts in a similar way to the ITC but for radio. Licenses and regulates commercial radio, monitors output and ensures obligations are met. Also regulates programming and advertising.

Public Service Broadcasters

BBC
Broadcasting House
London W1A 1AA
Director General: Greg Dyke.

The BBC has a multitude of different departments dealing with everything from network television, to local radio in the national regions, to selling soft toys of Pudsey the bear through BBC World-wide. The full addresses of the various sections of the BBC follow later, but below are the essential recruitment details:

For general recruitment enquiries:

For work experience enquiries:

BBC Recruitment
PO Box 7000
London W1A 8GJ
0870 333 1330
www.bbc.co.uk

BBC Recruitment
Work Experience
PO Box 27118
London W1A 6ZL
020 7765 5535
www.bbc.co.uk/workexperience
workexperience@bbc.co.uk

BBC Jobs Web Site
www.bbc.co.uk/jobs

Ceefax
Page 696 on BBC 1 and BBC 2
for current job vacancies.

The BBC in-house magazine, *Ariel*, includes job adverts. You can
subscribe by writing to:

Ariel Subscriptions
PO Box 324
Griffin House
Aylesbury
Buckinghamshire HP19 3BP
www.bbc.co.uk/info/bbc/ariel.shtml

BBC Television – Regions

BBC North
New Broadcasting House
Oxford Road
Manchester M60 1SJ

Broadcasting Centre
Woodhouse Lane
Leeds LS2 9PX

Broadcasting Centre
Barrack Road
Newcastle upon Tyne
NE99 2NE

BBC Midlands and East
Broadcasting Centre
Pebble Mill Road
Birmingham B5 7QQ

East Midlands Broadcasting Centre
York House
Mansfield Road
Nottingham NG1 3JB

St Catherine's Close
All Saints Green
Norwich
Norfolk NR1 3ND

BBC South
Broadcasting House
Whiteladies Road
Bristol BS8 2LR

Broadcasting House
Havelock Road
Southampton SO1 0XQ

Broadcasting House
Seymour Road
Mannamead
Plymouth PL3 5BD

Elstree Centre
Clarendon Road
Borehamwood
Hertfordshire WD6 1JF

BBC Wales
Broadcasting House
Llandaff
Cardiff CF5 2YQ

BBC Scotland
Broadcasting House
Queen Margaret Drive
Glasgow G12 8DG

BBC Northern Ireland
Broadcasting House
Ormeau Avenue
Belfast BT2 8HQ

National Radio

BBC Radio 1
Egton House
London W1A 1AA

BBC Radio 2, 3, 4, 5 live
Broadcasting House
London W1A 1AA

BBC World Service
PO Box 76
Bush House
Strand
London WC2B 4PH

BBC Local Radio

BBC 3 Counties Radio (Beds, Herts, Bucks)
PO Box 3CR
Hastings Street
Luton
Bedfordshire LU1 5XL

BBC Radio Berkshire
Broadcasting House
42a Portman Road
Reading RG3 1NB

BBC Radio Bristol
3 Tyndalls Park Road
Bristol BS8 1PP

BBC Radio Cambridgeshire
PO Box 96
104 Hills Road
Cambridge CB2 1LD

BBC Radio Cleveland
PO Box 95 FM
Middlesborough
Cleveland TS1 5DG

BBC Radio Cornwall
Phoenix Wharf
Truro TR1 1UA

BBC Radio Cumbria
Annetwell Street
Carlisle CA1 2NA

BBC CWR
25 Warwick Road
Coventry CV1 2WR

BBC Radio Derby
PO Box 269
Derby DE1 3HL

BBC Radio Devon
PO Box 100
St David's Hill
Exeter EX4 4DB

BBC Radio Essex
198 New London Road
Chelmsford CM2 9XB

BBC Radio Foyle
8 Northland Road
Derry
Northern Ireland BT48 7JT

BBC Radio Gloucestershire
London Road
Gloucester GL1 1SW

BBC Radio GLR
35c Marylebone High Street
London W1A 4LG

BBC Radio GMR
New Broadcasting House
PO Box 951
Oxford Roada
Manchester M60 1SD

BBC Radio Guernsey
Commerce House
Les Banques
St Peter Port
Guernsey Channel Islands

BBC Radio Hereford and Worcester
42 Broad Street
Hereford HR4 9HH

BBC Radio Humberside
9 Chapel Street
Hull NU1 3NU

BBC Radio Jersey
18 Parade Road
St Helier
Jersey
Channel Islands

BBC Radio Kent
Sun Pier
Chatham
Kent ME4 4EZ

BBC Radio Lancashire
Darwen Street
Blackburn
Lancashire BB2 2EA

BBC Radio Leeds
Broadcasting House
Woodhouse Lane
Leeds LS2 9PN

BBC Radio Leicester
Epic House
Charles Street
Leicester LE1 3SH

BBC Radio Lincolnshire
PO Box 219
Newport
Lincoln LN1 3XY

BBC Radio Merseyside
55 Paradise Street
Liverpool L1 3BP

BBC Radio Newcastle
Broadcasting Centre
Barrack Road
Newcastle upon Tyne
NE99 1RN

BBC Radio Norfolk
Norfolk Tower
Surrey Street
Norwich NR1 3PA

BBC Radio Northampton
Compton House
Abington Street
Northampton NN1 2BH

BBC Radio Nottingham
York House
Mansfield Road
Nottingham NG1 3JB

BBC Radio Oxford
269 Banbury Road
Oxford OX2 7DW

BBC Radio Peterborough
PO Box 957
Peterborough PE1 1YT

BBC Radio Sheffield
Ashdell Grove
60 Westbourne Road
Sheffield S10 2QU

BBC Radio Shropshire
2–4 Boscobel Drive
Shrewsbury SY1 3T

BBC Radio Solent
Broadcasting House
10 Havelock Road
Southampton SO1 0XR

BBC Somerset Sound
14–15 Paul Street
Taunton
Somerset TA1 3PF

BBC Radio Suffolk
Broadcasting House
St Matthew's Street
Ipswich IP1 3EP

BBC Radio Sussex and Surrey
Broadcasting House
Guildford Surrey GU2 5AP

BBC Radio Ulster
Ormeau Avenue
Belfast BT2 8HQ

BBC Wiltshire Sound
Broadcasting House
Prospect Place
Swindon
Wiltshire SN1 3RW

BBC Radio WM/WCR
PO Box 206
Pebble Mill Road
Birmingham B5 7SD

BBC Radio York
20 Bootham Row
York YO3 7BR

The Open University

The Open University output is part of the BBC's Learning Zone. It makes programmes such as *Rough Science*, which is *Challenge Anneka* meets *Wild Weather*! Each week Kate Humble and her team of five scientists are given three days to complete a given challenge. This sort of programming is perfect if you have a degree you want to make use of in a direct way. Tasks set are along the lines of finding a way to communicate across their Caribbean Island base and building an underwater light to examine marine life – all done using natural available resources.

For family education and information, there are such shows as *Mother Knows Best*, which looks at points of concern for families and discusses those issues with two sets of parents. Subjects may include the MMR vaccine, drugs and teenage pregnancies. A perfect show for someone with a family preparing to go into television, to work in research or similar fields.

The OU programmes are an amazing source of employment for those with a particular educational qualification.

Commercial Broadcasters

Commercial Television

ITV Network Centre
100 Gray's Inn Road
London WC1 8XZ
www.itv.com
Director of Programmes: Nigel Pickard

This body looks after the commissioning and scheduling for the whole of the ITV network. With the amalgamation of many of the ITV franchises into one company, the shape of its activities might change during 2003. Individual ITV companies are listed below

The network centre also has a number of commissioning controllers who look after specialist genres such as Drama, Factual and Daytime, etc.

ITV Companies
Anglia Television
Anglia House
Norwich NR1 3JG
www.angliatv.com

Border Television
Television Centre
Carlisle CA1 3NT
www.border-tv.com

Carlton Television
101 St Martin's
London WC2N 4AZ
www.carlton.com

Central Independent Television
Central House
Birmingham B1 2JP
www.itv.com/carltoncentral

Channel Television
The TV Centre
La Pouquelaye
St Helier
Jersey
Channel Islands

GMTV
The London Television Centre
Upper Ground
London SE1 9LT
www.gmtv.co.uk

Grampian Television
Queens Cross
Aberdeen AB9 2XJ
www.grampiantv.com

Granada Television
Quay Street
Manchester M60 9EA
www.granadamedia.com

London Weekend Television
The London Television Centre
Upper Ground
London SE1 9LT
www.lwt.co.uk

Meridian Broadcasting
Television Centre
Southampton SO2 0TA
www.meridiantv.com

Scottish Television
Cowcaddens
Glasgow G2 3PR
www.scottishtv.com

Tyne Tees Television
Television Centre
Newcastle Upon Tyne NE1 2AL
www.tynetees.tv

Ulster Television (UTV)
Havelock House
Ormeau Road
Belfast BT7 1EB
www.u.tv.com

Westcountry Television
Western Wood Way
Language Science Park
Plymouth
Devon PL7 5BG
www.itv.com/carltonwestcountry

Yorkshire Television
The Television Centre
Kirstal Road
Leeds LS3 1JS
www.yorkshire-television.tv

Channel 4
124 Horseferry Road
London SW1 2TX
www.Channel4.com

S4C
Sianel Pedwar Cymru
Parc Ty Glas
Llanshen
Cardiff CF4 5DV
www.s4c.com

Five
Channel 5 Broadcasting Limited
22 Long Acre
London WC2E 9LY
020 7550 5555
www.channel5.co.uk

Commercial Radio

National Radio Stations

Classic FM
Classic FM House
7 Swallow Place
London W1R 7AA
www.classicfm.com

TalkSport 1089/1053
PO BOX 1089
London SE1 8WQ
www.talksport.net

Virgin 1215
1 Golden Squae
London W1R 4DJ
www.virgin.com/radio

Talk Radio UK
76 Oxford Street
London W1N 0TR

Local Radio Stations

Bath FM 107.9
Station House
Ashley Avenue
Lower Weston
Bath BA1 3DS
www.bathfm.co.uk

Beacon 97.2
267 Tattenhall Road
Wolverhampton WV6 0DQ
www.koko.co.uk

The Bear 102.0
The Old Guard House Studios
Banbury Road
Stratford Upon Avon CV37 7HX
www.thebear.co.uk

BCR Fm 107.4
PO Box 1074
Bridgewater TA6 4WE
www.bcrfm.co.uk

BIG 1170 am
Stoke Road
Stoke on Trent ST4 2SR
www.big1170.co.uk

Bright 106.4
The Market Place Shopping
Centre
Burgess Hill
Wash Sussex RH1 9NP
www.bright1064.com

BRMB 96.4
9 Brindley Place
4 Oozells Square
Birmingham B1 2DJ
www.brmb.co.uk

Capital Fm 95.8
30 Leicester Square
London WC2H 7LA
www.capitalfm.com

Capital Gold 1152 am
9 Brindley Place
4 Oozells Square
Birmingham B1 2DJ
www.capitalgold.com

Centre FM 101.6
5–6 Aldergate
Tamworth
West Midlands B79 7DJ
www.centrefm.com

Century 106
City Link
Nottingham NG2 4NG
www.centuryfm.co.uk

Chiltern Radio 97.6
Chiltern Road
Dunstable
Bedfordshire LU6 1HQ
www.koko.co.uk

Chiltern Radio 96.9
55 Goldington Road
Bedford MK40 3LT
www.koko.co.uk

Connect fm 97.2
Unit 1
Centre 2000
Kettering
Northamptonshire NN16 8PU
www.connectfm.co.uk

County Sound 1566 AM
Dolphin House
North Street
Guildford GU1 4AA
www.countysound.co.uk

Delta FM 97.1
65 Weyhill
Haslemere
Surrey GU27 1HN
www.countysound.co.uk

The Eagle 96.4
Dolphin House
North Street
Guildford GU1 4AA
www.964eagle.co.uk

The Falcon 107.2
Brunel Mall
London Road
Stroud GL5 2BP
www.thefalcon.org

The Fire 107.6
PO Box 1234
Bournemouth BH1 2AO
www.clickhere.net

Fosseway Radio 107.9
PO Box 107
Hinckley LE10 1WR
www.fossewayradio.co.uk

Fox FM 102.6
Brush House
Pony Road
Oxford OX4 2XR
www.foxfm.co.uk

Fusion Radio 107.9
Suite 41
Westgate Centre
Oxford OX1 1PD
www.fusion1079.com

Galaxy 102.2
1 The Square
111 Broad Street
Birmingham
B15 1AS
www.galaxy1022.co.uk

Galaxy 101 97.2
Millennium House
26 Baldwin Street
Bristol BS1 1SE
www.galaxy101.com

GWR 96.3
PO Box 2000
One Passenger Street
Bristol BS99 7SN
www.koko.co.uk

GWR 96.5
PO Box 2000
Swindon SN4 7EX
www.koko.co.uk

Gemini FM
Hawthorn House
Exeter Business Park
Exeter EX1 3QS
www.koko.co.uk

Heart FM 100.7
1 The Square
111 Broad Street
Birmingham
BI5 1AS
www.heart1007.co.uk

Hertbeat 106.7
Hertbeat
Knebworth Park
Hertfordshire SG3 6HA
www.hertbeat.com

Horizon 103.3
14 Vincent Avenue
Milton Keynes MK8 0AB
www.koko.co.uk

Kestrel FM 107.6
Paddington House
The Walks
Basingstoke RG21 7LG
www.kestrel.co.uk

Kick Fm 105.6
The Studios
42 Bone Lane
Newbury RG14 5SO
www.kickfm.com

Kiss 100
Mappin House
4 Winsley Street
London W1W 8HF
www.kissfm.com

Kix 96.2
Watch Close
Spoon Street
Coventry CV1 3LN
www.kix.fm

Lantern 96.2
26 Lauder Lane
Roundswell Business Park
Barnstable EX31 3TA
www.koko.co.uk

Leicester Sound 105.4
6 Dominus Way
Meridian Business Park
Leicester LE19 1RR
www.koko.co.uk

Lincs FM 96.7
Witham Park
Waterside South
Lincoln LN5 7JN
www.lincsfm.co.uk

Mercia FM 97.0
Hertford Pace
Coventry CV1 3TT
www.koko.co.uk

Mix 96 96.2
Friars Square Studios
11 Bourbon Street
Aylesbury HP20 2PZ
www.mix96.co.uk

Northants 96.6
19–21 St Edmund's Road
Northampton NN1 5DY
www.koko.co.uk

107 Oak FM 107.0
7 Waldron Court
Loughborough LE11 5GD
www.oakfm.com

Oceon FM 96.7
Radio House
Whittle Avenue
Segensworth West
Fareham PO15 5SH
www.ocoenfm.com

Orchard FM 96.5
Haygrove House
Taunton TA3 7BT
www.koko.co.uk

Pirate FM 102.2
Carn Brea Studios
Wilson Way
Redruth TR15 3XX
www.piratefm102.co.uk

Plymouth Sound 96.6
Earls Avenue
Plymouth PL3 4MX
www.koko.co.uk

Power FM 103.2
Radio House
Whittle Avenue
Segensworth West
Fareham PO15 5SH
www.powerfm.com

The Quay 107.4
PO Box 1074
Portsmouth PO2 8YG
www.quay radio.co.uk

Quay West 102.4
Harbour Studios
The Esplanade
Watchet TA23 0AJ

Radio XL 1296 FM
KMS House
Bradford Street
Birmingham B12 0JO

Ram fm 102.8
35–36 Irongate
Derby DE1 3GA
www.koko.co.uk

RugbyFM 107.1
4–6 Dunsmare Business Centre
Spring Street
Rugby CV21 3HH
www.rugby.fm

Rutland Radio 107.2
40 Melton Road
Oakham
Rutland LE15 6AY
www.rutnet.co.uk

Sabras 1260 am
Radio House
63 Melton Road
Leicester LE4 6PN
www.sabrasradio.co.uk

Saga 105.7
Crown House
Beaufort Court
123 Hagley Road
Birmingham B16 8LD
www.saga.co.uk/105.7fm

Saga 106.6
Huntingdon House
278–290 Huntingdon Street
Nottingham NG1 3LY
www.saga.co.uk/106.6fm

Severn Sound 102.4
Bridge Studios
Eastgate Centre
Gloucester GL1 13S
www.koko.co.uk

Signal 1 96.9
Stoke Road
Stoke on Trent ST4 2SR
www.signal1.co.uk

South City fm
City Studios
Marsh Lane
Southampton SO14 3ST
www.southcityfm.co.uk

South Hams Radio 100.5
Unit 9
South Hams Business Park
Churchstow
Kingsbridge TQ7 3QR

Spire FM 102.0
City Hall Studios
Malthoude Lane
Salisbury SP2 7QQ
www.spirefm.co.uk

Spirit FM 96.6
Dukes Court
Bognor Road
Chichester PO19 2FX
www.spiritfm.net

Star FM 106.6
The Observatory Shop Centre
Slough SL1 1LH
www.starfm.co.uk

Star 107.7
11 Beaconsfield Road
Weston-super-Mare BS23 1YE
www.star1077.co.uk

Star 107.5
West Suite
Arle Court
Hatherley Lane
Cheltenham GL51 6NP
www.star1075.co.uk

Star 107.3
Bristol Eve Post Building
Temple Way
Bristol BS99 7HD
www.star1075.co.uk

Sunshine 855 AM
Sunshine House
Waterside
Ludlow SY8 1PE

Swan fm 107.4
PO Box 107
High Wycombe
Buckinghamshire HO13 6WQ

Telfora FM 107.4
PO Box 1074
Telford TF3 3WG
www.telfordfm.co.uk

96 Trent FM 96.2
29–31 Castle Gate
Nottingham NG1 7AP

Wessex FM 96.0
Radio House
Trinity Street
Dorchester DT1 1DJ
www.wessexfm.co.uk

The Wolf 107.7
10 Floor
Mander House
Wolverhampton WV1 3NB
www.thewolf.co.uk

Wyvern FM 96.7
5–6 Barbourne Terrace
Worcester WR1 3JZ

3TR FM 107.5
Riverside Studios
Warminster BA12 9HQ
www.3tr.com

2Cr FM 102.3
5 Southcote Road
Bournemouth BH1 3LR
www.koko.co.uk

Internet Radio Stations

Afrozic: French: African music
www.afrozic.net

Funradio: France: pop music
www.funradio.fr/home.asp

Lycos: US: Variety music
www.music.lycos.com/rhapsody

Industry Organizations

The Royal Television Society
The RTS has regional centres, all of which host lectures, often open to the public, all over the UK and US. The Television Society was formed in 1927, nine years before the first public service broadcast from Alexandra Palace. The RTS is the only Society exclusively devoted to television and, as the industry undergoes significant change, it stands as a central independent forum where the art, business and politics of television can be discussed by representatives from every branch of the industry.

RTS North America Inc. was founded in the 1980s to serve members in the States. The Society's Head Office, based in London, organizes many events; you can contact them to discover if anything is happening near you.

The Royal Television Society
Holborn Hall
100 Gray's Inn Road
London WC1X 8AL
020 7430 1000
Fax: 020 7430 0924
www.rts.org.uk

The AIB: Association for International Broadcasting
Thousands of hours of international radio and television programmes
are broadcast each week, in many different languages. The Association
for International Broadcasting sees this complex, interlocking output
as a single network, spreading news and information to the whole
planet. The AIB aims to increase the scope and effectiveness of
international broadcasting, working on a global, co-operative basis.
The AIB:

- encourages co-operation within and throughout the international
  broadcasting industry
- provides the industry with news and information about international broadcasting
- provides the means for worldwide publicity of available services
  and products
- promotes development and high standards within international
  broadcasting
- speaks for the whole of international broadcasting
- promotes international broadcasting to increase the public's
  knowledge base.

AIB
PO Box 990
London SE3 9XL
www.aib.org.uk

PACT – Producers Alliance for Cinema and TV
PACT was founded in 1991 and runs as the trade association in the
UK. It represents independent television, animation and interactive and
new media production companies. The bulk of PACT's resources are
dedicated to providing a comprehensive range of production-related
services to help members in their daily business. They also encourage
the development of new production companies and producers.
The PACT handbook is available from:

Gordon House
10 Greencoat Place
London SW1P 1PH
www.pact.co.uk

Short Courses

PACT holds a variety of short courses and events with a training focus on business, legal and copyright issues. Most of these are for members only, although occasionally they are open to non-members. Details of course content, times and venues can be found in the events and training calendar on their web site.

Skills For Media

Skills For Media is a partnership between Skillset, which is an investment and research company, and BECTU (a trade union for media). The web site has advice for careers and training, workshops, etc.: www.skillsformedia.com/services

Skillset

2nd Floor
91–101 Oxford Street
London W1R 1RA
020 7534 5300
www.skillset.org

The Edinburgh International Television Festival

The Guardian Edinburgh International Television Festival (GEITF)
1st Floor
17–21 Emerald Street
London WC1N 3QN
020 7430 1333
Fax: 020 7430 2299
www.geitf.co.uk

Exchange Programmes

Radio Netherlands offer the opportunity for a UK student to gain a bursary to spend one month with the English Language Service in Hilversum, Holland.

Mike Shaw
Head of English Language Service
Radio Netherlands
Witte Kruislan 55
1200 JG Hilversum
The Netherlands

National Council for the Training of Journalists
Latton Bush Centre
Southern Way
Harlow
Essex CM18 7BL
www.holdthefrontpage.co.uk/training

Radio Academy

The Radio Academy has members from throughout the radio industry. It holds seminars and conferences and is responsible for the industry's annual conference. Its web site contains a great deal of information about courses and opportunities in the radio business.

Radio Academy
5 Market Place
London W1W 8AE
www.radioacademy.org

Student Radio Association
Radio Academy
5 Market Place London
W1W 8AE

News Organizations

ABC News International
8 Carburton Street
London W1P 7DT

CBS News UK
68 Knightsbridge
London SW1X 7LL

CNN International
CNN House
19–22 Rathbone Place
London W1P 1DF

Independent Radio News
1 Euston Centre
London NW1 3JG

ITN
Gray's Inn Road
London WC1X 8XZ

The London News Network
The London Television Centre
Upper Ground
London SE1 9LT

Sky News
6 Centaurs Business Park
Grant Way
Isleworth
Middlesex TW7 5QD

WTN Worldwide Television News
The Interchange
Oval Road
Camden Lock
London NW1

General Broadcasting Websites

American Federation of Television and Radio Artistes
www.aftra.org
www.archive.museophile.sbu.ac.uk
   Great links to broadcast institutions

Broadcast Now
www.broadcastnow.co.uk
   TV and radio industry web site, including news, jobs, archives, etc.

Press Gazette
www.pressgazette.co.uk
   UK Press Gazette online, good media and journalism information.

Media Circle
www.mediacircle.co.uk
   Graduate jobs and media information.

Your Creative Future
www.yourcreativefuture.org.uk
   Information and good advice on jobs in new media, TV, film and radio.

Commercial Radio Companies Association
www.crca.co.uk
   Advice and work placements database.

Commercial Production Companies
Commercial Production
Complete Production
www.completeproduction.com

Courses

BTEC National Award in Media
One year course
Lambeth College
020 7501 5555

Presenting Courses
Ranging from one day to three, some with showreels, some without.

All the below offer pieces to camera, interview techniques and autocue training, etc.

MediaMania
One day courses with or without showreel.
Cambridge
01223 237700
Fax: 01223 235870
www.mediamania.co.uk

Courses in presenting and speech training, etc. based at the London Drama School.
www.london-drama-school.co.uk
www.startek-uk.com

www.positiv.com/televisionpresenters
One Day Presenting course with showreel; based in Berkshire. Good reputation.

www.media-master.co.uk

Getting into presenting
www.smmp.salford.ac.uk/imc/shortcourses
   3 day course, no showreel.

The Institute of Music and Technology
www.imthurricane.org
   Courses in new media and radio techniques

Useful Publications

The Blue Book of British Broadcasting
Tellex Monitors
47 Gray's Inn Road
London WC1X 8PR

National Press Advertising
The more commonly used print media include:

Guardian (Monday, with a repeat on Saturday)
Daily Telegraph (Thursday)
Broadcast (Friday)
The Sunday Times

The Radio Magazine
Crown House
25 High Street
Rothwell
Kettering NN14 6AD
www.theradiomagazine.co.uk
info@theradiomagazine.co.uk

Competitions

Sneaky ways into journalism! There are plenty of competitions for struggling young journalists, often with prizes of jobs, experience and published work. The *York Evening Press* runs a yearly competition called Write Stuff. The winner gets a job with the paper after completing a funded course in journalism. Many local newspapers run such competitions to find and nurture new talent. Check out your local paper to discover whether they have any such opportunities. If they don't there's no reason why you can't suggest it to them...

The same opportunities exist for budding young photographers. *The Times*/Tabasco 'Young Photographer of the Year' competition is an annual competition, with the winner receiving a six-month paid contract at *The Times*.

William Randolph Hearst Foundation Journalism Awards
www.hearstfdn.org
   Competitions for undergraduates in radio, TV news and journalism.

ABSW
www.absw.org.uk/awards
   Writing awards, especially for science writing.

Glossary

acquisition purchasing shows for broadcast, as opposed to making them yourself.

ADSL high speed communications link, similar to ISDN.

air play the time given to playing a record 'on air'.

A list top celebrities.

AM Amplitude Modulation – an analogue form of radio transmission, using signal variation to create sound.

analogue land-based signal transmitters.

announcements a pre-prepared piece of transmitted speech.

as live broadcast to seem live when actually pre-recorded.

autocue pilot negative name for newscasters.

back ref radio: reference to a song just played.

bandwidth space on a radio transmission spectrum.

BJTC British Journalists Training Council

blocking selecting a portion of script to associate with an action in a programme.

breaking story news just arriving.

broadband method of carrying a digital transmission.

broken (news) story which has already been broadcast.

buffering delay while downloading live material from the Internet.

bulletins individual news stories grouped together into a single (main) news broadcast. Shorter version described as 'summary' or 'headlines'.

cadence ways in which a voice can be varied.

cap gen caption generator.

cast type how you appear to others.

CD ROM production programme recorded onto a CD disk, usually interactive.

CEO Chief Executive Officer (of a company).

client list list of people on an agent's books.

commission buying a show from a producer to broadcast.

commissioning process stages of buying a show from a producer.

console a piece of 'furniture' holding technical equipment, usually a sound or vision mixing desk.

constructed montages pieces of video action cut together, often to music.

continuity announcer person who helps to bridge gaps between programmes with speech, giving interesting and relevant information.

convergence the coming together of different methods of distributing information or programmes, using the same piece of equipment to perform different tasks. For example, a computer carrying television pictures and receiving faxes and telephone calls.

cover letter letter to accompany a CV, introducing the applicant.

cuttings articles from newspapers or magazines.

CV Curriculum Vitae – a list of your experience and employment.

DAB Digital Audio Broadcasting (digital radio).

DAT Digital Audio Tape.

day part sections of a broadcasting day. Often used to describe the time when a DJ performs on air.

dedication a song dedicated to a particular person, often requested for a loved one.

desks radio broadcast equipment often embedded in furniture – see *console*.

digital a form of transmission using binary (computer-like) signals.

digital TV platforms transmission devices for digital signals, sometimes satellites, etc.

dish farm a group of satellite dishes able to receive and transmit TV and radio signals.

DTG Digital Television Group. Industry advisory body.

down the line sending programme material from a remote studio to the main broadcast centre. Often used to describe a remote interview.

download to receive data (into a computer or radio/radio set).

drive the desk controlling a programme with a mixing desk.

drop in piece of music or recorded speech material 'dropped in' to a programme e.g. a station identity jingle used as a tune is ending.

DVB Digital Video Broadcast.

ear piece device inserted in the ear to enable communication between individuals. Often used by producers or directors to talk to broadcast presenters.

ENG Electronic News Gathering.

eyeline an individual's line of sight – the direction a person is looking (towards a camera).

fact-based narrative commentary using factual information.

fades out turning volume down on music, often as the presenter speaks over the last few bars.

feedback howling sound when sound signals interact on themselves.

final cut final production of a programme.

flagship usually refers to a signature show: the 'jewel in the crown' of a broadcast company.

flying hours time spent behind a microphone – 'Air Miles'

FM Frequency Modulation – Analogue method of radio transmission, using variations in frequency to create sound.

footprint reception area of satellite transmissions.

format structure (of programmes).

franchise auction licences to broadcast sold to the highest bidder.

freelance worker independent of an organization or company – often self-employed.

frontline where the action is; where the story is breaking.

gallery control room of a broadcasting studio.

gaming design and production of computer games.

generic specific to one genre.

genres specific areas of designation. In broadcasting, e.g. History, News or Children's programmes.

geography the spatial make up of the studio.

geo-stationary satellites hovering in a static position above the earth.

guidelines instructions on how to conduct broadcasts, e.g. to remain impartial.

hard end song ending (then the presenter speaks).

Harry graphic editing machine.

hooks descriptions of things to come (to keep a listener interested in a programme).

house style the method, style or fashion in which a company likes material to be constructed, e.g. a way of speaking or behaving.

HTML HyperText Markup Language – code used in web site design.

hypertext Abbreviation for HTML material.

ILR Independent Local Radio.

imagineering designing a piece of entertainment or equipment that does not currently exist, and which is often completely fictitious.

in house production created within the company that will broadcast it.

intake area for gathering material, usually news, into a broadcast centre.

interactivity ability of viewers/listeners to exchange information with a broadcaster.

interactive multimedia devices, using all forms of media information, which can be interrogated to deliver sound and vision in various forms, e.g. a CD encyclopaedia or computer game.

interactive platforms devices which enable interactivity.

interactive TV programmes which enable viewers to participate in a programme or select desired video material.

interactive web interactivity using the Internet.

internships posts (usually unpaid) which give the holder experience of a working environment.

intranet internal computer network system, used by large companies.

iris wipe a special effect from a television mixing desk.

IRN Independent Radio News

ISDN high speed communication link, similar to ADSL.

ITN Independent Television News.

IT skills information technology abilities.

ITV Independent Television.

jingle message with music, sometimes played as radio station identification.

links presentation between items or programmes to ensure smooth continuity.

listings TV schedules in magazines and newspapers.

live programme programme produced as it is broadcast.

location expert person skilled in selecting filming sites.

media all forms of devices used to carry information – newspapers, television, etc.

multi-skilled individual who can undertake multiple tasks.

multiple duty one person doing several jobs, e.g. reporting, researching and editing: multi-skilling.

multiplexers chain of digital transmitters.

NCTJ National Council for the Training of Journalists.

networking the art of meeting important people.

news agencies companies collating news to sell to media.

news images news illustrations added from library or agency sources.

news makers people involved with a news story.

news sense ability to spot an interesting news story.

news sources people or organizations who supply news to broadcasters.

newsroom area set aside for the production of news programmes.

offline viewing a way to view material using nontransmission equipment.

old media terrestrial TV, analogue broadcasting, newspapers.

on air broadcasting.

on the road reporting from an outside location.

online journalism web-based journalism.

opt out replacement of a programme being broadcast by a more local programme.

outside broadcast programme broadcast outside of the studio.

packages assembled news reports.

PACT Producers Alliance for Cinema and TV.

pan-galactic gargle blaster drink, as illustrated in *The Hitchhiker's Guide to the Galaxy*!

patch slang for specific area or subject covered by an individual or team.

PD programme director.

picture construction composition of a video image or scene.

picture depth quality and range of visual subject.

piece to camera monologue from presenter delivered to the camera.

platforms specific means or device of delivery (of a transmission).

playlist list of tunes to be played on a particular station.

portable audio recording equipment tape recorder.

portal 'gateway' to a particular transmission, as in an address of a web page.

portfolio group of similar items or programmes gathered together in one collection.

positive copy final print of film taken from an edited negative.

post production production work done on a programme after it has been taped or filmed (usually by way of editing or the addition of effects).

PR public relations.

pre-recording carries jingle and standard radio information.

presenting hosting a show for the audience at home.

press releases infomation about a show that is given to the press to publish.

production the realization of an idea into a product, e.g. a broadcast programme.

production credits list of people responsible for a production (usually shown at the end of a programme).

production process route by which a production or programme has to be taken in order to reach transmission stage.

production unit group of people and resources capable of producing a programme.

programme output style of or specific programmes broadcast by a particular company

programming languages software or design programmes such as HTML.

programming techniques skills used in making programmes.

promoted advertised.

PTC presenter speaking directly to camera – piece to camera.

public service broadcaster a broadcaster serving the public interests with no personal agenda or need for profit.

reads whole story read to camera by the presenter alone.

recall audition call back

regional broadcaster broadcaster/presenter who works in one region.

regulatory bodies organizations such as the ITC and OFCOM.

rehearsal room rooms used for rehearsals and auditions.

requests request for the playing of a particular musical tune – see *dedication*.

rip 'n' read teleprinted, faxed or e-mailed text which can be broadcast without editing – usually news.

road show radio broadcast from outside the studio.

ROT Record of Transmission.

rotate placement of shows in the schedule.

running order how things work within a programme.

satellite device outside the earth's atmosphere, used in broadcasting as a transmitter of radio/TV signals back to earth.

scanning eye movement (such as when reading an autocue).

schedules the timetable for the transmission of programmes.

scripts paper or electronic instructions on what is said and shown in a broadcast programme.

segue two songs played back-to-back on radio, without interruption.

self-introduction part of social networking: pushing self forward without becoming annoying.

sequence programmes programmes which run before or after each other in a designed structure.

set scenery within which a production takes place.

set top box facility to accesses channels and interactivity.

sharing agreements news companies in different countries exchanging news items.

shift leader person in charge of a team during work shift.

shots individual groups of pictures.

showreel examples of on-air experience, a video or audio CV.

signature sound type of music played by a radio station.

Sky BSkyB Ltd., a satellite TV network, part of News Corporation.

SMS way of sending text messages, usually to mobile phones.

SNG satellite news gathering.

software packages digital material to create computer programmes.

spectrum platform on which channels are broadcast.

station ID the specific identification signal, sometimes music, of a broadcaster.

steadicam gyroscopically controlled camera that smooths out the visual effect of bumps and other visual disturbance.

Steinbeck brand name of a film-editing machine.

streamed/streaming the method of transmission of moving pictures and sound on the Internet.

striking dismantling a studio set.

studio floor technical name for place where programmes are recorded.

sunrise newsroom newsroom which is part of a group, sharing the worldwide transmission of news on a 24-hour basis. Each component newsroom broadcasts for a section of the clock, usually eight hours.

sweep many tunes played back-to-back on the radio.

talking heads see *autocue pilot*.

talent the industry speak for on-air performers.

TC/TVC the BBC's Television Centre.

TCP/IP internet address system.

template structures design for standardizing the order of things.

terrestrial broadcasting using land-based transmitters – as opposed to satellites.

texting SMS text messages sent primarily by mobile phone.

tracks career paths, usually two: on air and production.

trainee person employed to learn the trade.

transmission the onward relay of a broadcast signal to receivers.

transmission fault a problem which prevents transmission.

transponders transmitters mounted on satellites.

TV licence compulsory fee paid in order to receive TV and radio.

undercover secret gathering of news information.

uplinked transmission of a broadcast signal to a satellite transponder.

VJs video jockey.

voice over unseen presentation of a narration (usually to a programme or programme item).

Vortals slang name for an Internet portal carrying video transmissions.

VT video tape.

web site operators companies and individuals controlling Internet pages.

webcasting broadcasting specifically on the web.

wires slang for telegraph signals which carry news stories around the world.

wire services international news agencies selling stories from around the world, via various delivery methods.

work experience time spent at a company to learn about the business, usually unpaid.

worked up a news story which is treated to further research.

zoo format a group involved in one broadcast show interacting on air.

Feedback

The business of broadcasting is an organic one. Disciplines, techniques and technology are changing almost every day. I freely acknowledge that parts of this book may need updating before long.

I need the help of everyone in keeping the information bang up-to-date and, apart from professionals already in the broadcasting game, it would be useful to hear the views and anecdotes of people who are trying to get into it – especially for the first time.

I am also aware, as I say several times in this book, that people need advice specific to their own situation.

Readers and others should feel free to contact me with questions, further advice and any other material for future editions. My address is:

Mike Hollingsworth
Venture Artistes
PO Box 299
Oxford OX2 6LN
venture-artistes@msn.com

People asking for specific replies may be asked to defray expenses, and should also enclose a stamped, addressed, envelope.

Thank you for buying the book – and good luck with your career. May our paths cross at the highest level!

Index